D1470244

NATO MAJOR WARSHIPS — USA & CANADA

A Tri-Service Pocketbook

The Tri-Service Pocketbook Series

The Air Series
NATO Major Combat Aircraft
Soviet and East European Major Combat Aircraft
Commercial Transport Aircraft
Military Transport and Training Aircraft
World Helicopters
World Light Aircraft

The Military Series
Battlefield Close Air Support
Artillery Systems
Soft-Skinned Military Vehicles
Main Battle Tanks
APCs and MCVs
Light Tanks, Armoured Cars and Reconnaissance Vehicles
Anti-Tank Systems
Air Defence Systems
Pistols and Rifles
Machine Guns and Submachine Guns
Battlefield Electronic Systems
Battlefield Mobility Equipment
Infantry Support Systems
Bomb Disposal, Detection and Anti-Riot Equipment
Surveillance and Perimeter Protection Equipment
Internal Security Vehicles
Communications Equipment
Battlefield Counter Mobility Equipment
Repair and Recovery Vehicles

The Naval Series
NATO Major Warships — Europe
NATO Major Warships — USA and Canada
Soviet and East European Major Warships
Major Warships — Asia, Africa, Australasia and
Latin America
The World's Small Warships

NATO MAJOR WARSHIPS — USA & CANADA

Eric J. Grove

A Tri-Service Pocketbook

TRI-SERVICE

PRESS

First published by Tri-Service Press Limited, 42/43 Lower Marsh,
London SE1 7RQ, United Kingdom

British Library Cataloguing in Publication Data

Grove, Eric
    NATO major warships — USA and Canada
    1. North Atlantic Treaty Organisation navies. Warships.
    I. Title
    623.825091821

    ISBN 1-85488-020-9

Distribution in the United States by Howell Press, Inc.,
700 Harris Street, Suite B, Charlottesville, Virginia 22901.
Telephone (804) 977-4006.

Typeset by Florencetype Ltd, Kewstoke, Avon
Printed in the United Kingdom

Notes on tables
Dimensions: length is always given overall.
Torpedoes: HWT heavyweight torpedo, LWT lightweight torpedo
Sonar: low frequency is below 3 kHz, medium frequency 3–10 k
    high frequency above 10 kHz.
Radar Bands: E 2–3 gHz, F 3–4 gHz, G 4–6 gHz, H 6–9 gHz,
    I 9–10, J 10–20 gHz.

Introduction

is pocketbook completes the coverage of the navies of the Atlantic
lance in the Tri-Service Pocketbook series. The Canadian Navy is
rrently undergoing much-needed modernisation. This will allow it to
aintain its important contribution to the NATO Striking Fleet.

The United States Navy remains the most powerful in the world, but
undergoing significant contraction. Older submarines are being
leted when they require reactor refuelling. As decommissioned
bmarines never go to sea again they have not been included on the
lowing pages.

The US Navy is also reducing its surface forces. The number of
rrier battle groups has been reduced from 15 to 14 and battleship
rface action groups from 4 to 2. The Atlantic-based Second Fleet is
ing the brunt of the cuts, losing a carrier battle group (CVBG) and a
rface action group (SAG) from its wartime deployment. This leaves
ee CVBGs for the Second Fleet, five CVBGs and an SAG for the
venth Fleet in the Western Pacific/Indian Ocean, two CVBGs for the
rd Fleet in the Eastern Pacific and four CVBGs for the Sixth Fleet in
e Mediterranean. Surface escorts are also being reduced. As
commissioned carriers and surface vessels are kept in reserve they
main listed in the following pages, along with reserve vessels that
re decommissioned some time ago.

As in the other titles in the series, conventional submarines are
ted after surface combatants and before amphibious vessels. The
larger cutters of the US Coast Guard which have an escort role in war
have been included as surface combatants. 'A' after a unit's name
indicates Atlantic deployment, and 'P' Pacific deployment.

Eric J. Grove is a well-known naval authority and historian, highly
regarded for his analytical expertise. In this series he brings together
all his experience and contacts to provide the very latest information on
the world's in-service navies. His other books are: *Vanguard to
Trident: British Naval Policy Since World War II*; *The Future of Sea
Power*; *Sea Battles in Close-up*; *NATO's Defence of the North*. He
has held appointments as Civilian Lecturer, RN College Dartmouth,
1971–84 (Deputy Director of Strategic Studies 1982–4), Exchange
Professor USN Annapolis, 1980–81, worked with the Council for
Arms Control, 1985–6; since 1986 freelance defence writer and
consultant; helped establish the Foundation for International Security,
of which he is now the Naval Research Director.

Author's acknowledgments: Thanks to Dr and Mrs G.E.B. Grove for
assistance with compilation and word processing, and to Linda Cullen
and Mary Beth Straight of the US Naval Institute and David Foxwell of
Naval Forces for help with pictures.

Abbreviations

A	Atlantic deployment *(after vessel name)*
AAW	anti-air warfare
ACIS	amphibious command information system
ADLIPS	automatic data link plotting system
ADCAP	advanced capability
AEW	airborne early warning
ADGE	escort research ship
AGF	miscellaneous command ship
AGFF	frigate research ship
AIO	action information organisation
AKA	attack cargo ship
ASROC	anti-submarine rocket
ASW	anti-submarine warfare
ATF	fleet tug
AVT	training auxiliary carrier
BB	battleship
CA	heavy cruiser
CANEWS	Canadian electronic warfare system
CANTASS	Canadian towed array sonar system
CCS	combat control system
CDS	combat data system/command and decision system
CG	guided missile cruiser
CGN	nuclear-powered guided missile carrier
CIWS	close-in weapons system
CVA	attack aircraft carrier
CVB	armoured aircraft carrier
CVAN	nuclear-powered attack aircraft carrier
CVN	nuclear-powered aircraft carrier
DASH	drone anti-submarine helicopter
DD	destroyer
DDG	guided missile destroyer
DDH	helicopter destroyer
DDS	dry deck shelter
DE	destroyer escort/ocean escort
DELEX	destroyer life extension program
DL	'frigate' (large destroyer)
DLG	guided missile 'frigate' (large destroyer)
DLGN	nuclear-powered guided missile 'frigate' (large destroyer)
ECM	electronic countermeasures
ER	extended range
ESM	electronic support measure (ie emissions receiver)
EW	electronic warfare
FF	frigate
FFG	guided missile frigate
FFH	helicopter frigate
FFISTS	frigate shipboard integrated data system
FRAM	fleet rehabilitation and modernisation program
HWT	heavyweight torpedo
LAMPS	light airborne multi-purpose system
LCAC	landing craft air cushion
LCC	amphibious command ship
LCM	mechanised landing craft

LCP	landing craft personnel		SCB	Ships Characteristics Board (numbering system)
LCU	utility landing craft		SCS	sea control ship
LCVP	landing craft vehicle and personnel		SEAL	Sea-Air-Land (US Navy Special Forces)
LHA	amphibious assault ship		SHINPADS	shipboard integrated processing and display system
LHD	amphibious assault ship		SLBM	submarine-launched ballistic missile
LKA	amphibious cargo ship		SLCM	sea-launched cruise missile
LPA	amphibious transport		SLEP	service life extension program
LPD	amphibious transport dock		SOUP	submarine operational update project
LPH	amphibious assault ship		SRBOC	super rapid-blooming off-board chaff
LSD	dock landing ship		SS	submarine (conventionally-powered)
LST	tank landing ship		SSM	surface-to-surface missile
LVT	landing vehicle tracked		SSBN	nuclear-powered ballistic missile submarine
LVTP	landing vehicle tracked personnel		SSN	nuclear-powered attack submarine
LWT	lightweight torpedo		STOV/L	short take off vertical landing
MMA	major maintenance availability		TASS	towed array sonar system
MR	medium range		TRUMP	Tribal update and modernisation program
NATO	North Atlantic Treaty Organisation		USS	United States Ship
NBCD	nuclear, biological and chemical defence		VDS	variable depth sonar
NIPS	naval intelligence processing system		VLS	vertical launch system
NRF	Naval Reserve Force		WAG	icebreaker
NTDS	naval tactical data system		WAGB	icebreaker
P	Pacific deployment (*after vessel name*)		WHEC	high endurance coast guard cutter
PAIR	performance and integration refit		WMEC	medium endurance coast guard cutter
PWR	pressurised water-cooled reactor		WPC	patrol craft
SALT	strategic arms limitation talks/treaty			
SAM	surface-to-air missile			

NATO MAJOR WARSHIPS — USA & CANADA

IROQUOIS DDH280 1972 A
HURON DDH281 1972 P
ATHABASKAN DDH282 1972 A
ALGONQUIN DDH283 1973 A

Specifications and Technical Data

Displacement, tonnes: 4,200 full load
Dimensions, metres (feet): 129.8 × 15.2 × 6.6
(426 × 50 × 21.5)
Aircraft: 2 × CH-124A Sea King ASW helicopters
Missiles: SAM: (modernised ships) 32 × Standard SM2-MR
Mk 41 vertical launch system forward; (unmodernised)
4 × 4 Sea Sparrow forward, 32 missiles
Guns: (modernised) 1 × 1 76 mm forward, 1 × 1 20 mm
Vulcan Phalanx CIWS on hangar roof; (unmodernised)
1 × 1 127 mm forward
Torpedoes: 2 × 3 324 mm for Mk 46 ASW LWT aft
A/S Weapons: 1 × 3 Limbo Mk 10 mortar (unmodernised
ships only)
Sonar: SQS 505 hull-mounted and variable depth medium-
frequency active, SQS 501 hull-mounted high-frequency
active target classification
Radar: (modernised) LW 08 D band air search DA 08 E/F
band surface search/navigaton STIR 1.8 I/J band fire control;
(unmodernised) SPS 501 D band air search SPQ 2D I band
surface search/navigation WM 22 I/J band fire control
Action Information Organisation: (modernised) SHINPADS;
(unmodernised) CCS-228
Machinery: 2 × Pratt & Whitney FT4A2 gas turbines,
50,000 hp; (modernised) 2 × GM Allison 570KF gas
turbines, 12,800 hp; (unmodernised) 2 × Pratt & Whitney
FT12AH3 gas turbines, 7,400 hp
Speed, knots: 29
Range, nautical miles: 4,500 at 20 knots
Complement: 285

A distinctively Canadian type of large anti-submarine
destroyer designed for the operation of large helicopters
using the Bear Trap landing system. In 1960 a programme of

eight 'Tribal' Class guided missile anti-aircraft frigates was
announced but this was cancelled in 1963 and the design
changed to emphasise ASW before four ships were ordered
in 1968. They were all laid down the following year, DDH280
and DDH281 at Marine Industries, Sorel and the rest at Davie
Shipbuilding Co., Lauzon. The first ships from each builder
were launched in November 1970 and the second in April
1971. They are currently being updated with new anti-aircraft
and gun armament, improved torpedo stowage and new
radar under the TRUMP (Tribal Update and Modernisation
Project). This was awarded to Litton Systems Canada in June
1988. DDH283 began reconstruction in November 1987. The
work suffered delays and will not be completed until late
1990. The rest of the class will be processed in the order
DDH280, DDH282 and DDH281. The work is being carried

out at the Davie yard and DDH280 is due to complete in early
1991. All four ships should be modernised by 1993. The
ships' EW systems will be modernised; Shield chaff
launchers will replace Corvus, CANEWS will replace the WLR
ESM and Ramses will replace the ULQ 6 jammer. DDH281
was fitted with CANEWS and Ramses before conversion. She
was deployed to the Pacific in 1987. The ships were
originally fitted with twin angled funnels to avoid aerial
corrosion. These are being replaced by a new single funnel
which will carry an infra-red signature suppressor.

Photograph: *Algonquin* (HM Steele)
Silhouette: 'Tribal' class as modernised

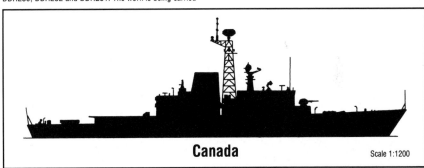

Canada

Scale 1:1200

1

Specifications and Technical Data

Displacement, tonnes: 3,063 full load
Dimensions, metres (feet): 113.1 × 12.8 × 4.4
(371 × 42 × 14.4)
Aircraft: 1 × CH-124A Sea King
Guns: 1 × 2 76 mm forward
Torpedoes: 2 × 3 324 mm Mk 32 tubes for
Mk 46 ASW LWT
Sonar: SQR 501 CANTASS low-frequency towed array,
SQS 505 hull-mounted medium-frequency active,
SQS 501 hull-mounted high-frequency active
Radar: SPS 503 E/F band air/surface search,
SPS 10 G band surface search, SPG 48 I/J band fire control
Action Information Organisation: ADLIPS
Machinery: 2 × English Electric geared turbines,
30,000 hp, 2 × shafts, 2 × Babcock & Wilcox
boilers
Speed, knots: 28
Range, nautical miles: 4,570 at 14 knots
Complement: 210

The final development of 'St. Laurent' class destroyer
escorts, these two ships were ordered in 1959 and laid
down in 1960, *Annapolis* at Halifax Shipyards Ltd.
in July and and *Nipigon* at Marine Industries Ltd., Sorel
in April. They were built to operate large Sea King ASW
helicopters by the Bear Trap technique, which the
Canadians pioneered at this time. A lighter American
3-inch Mk 33 forward gun mounting was chosen instead
of the previously used British Mk 6 to save topweight.

Annapolis was launched on 27 April 1963 and *Nipigon*
on 10 December 1961. They received their first
modernisation in 1977-79 and between 1982 and 1985
the two ships underwent an extensive DELEX (Destroyer
Life Extension Program) refit at a cost of Can $22 million
per ship. This involved fitting new action information
organisation, radar, sonar, communications and
electronic warfare equipment. The latter includes SRBOC
chaff rocket launchers and CANEWS ESM. The ships
were fitted with CANTASS towed array sonar in place
of their previous variable depth equipment in 1987-88.
This was a trials version of the system which is to be
replaced from 1991 by the definitive service equipment.
These ships are due to remain in service until the

mid-1990s but will probably last longer as they are very
useful towed array assets for the ASW Striking Force of
the NATO Striking Fleet.

Photograph: *Nipigon* (HM Steele)

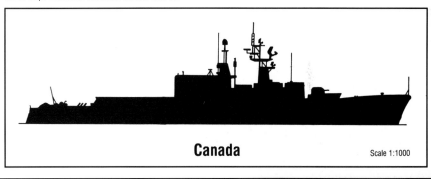

Canada

Scale 1:1000

SAGUENAY DDH206 A
SKEENA DDH207 A
OTTAWA DDH229 A
MARGAREE DDH230 A
FRASER DDH233 A

pecifications
ıd Technical Data

placement, tonnes: 3,051 full load
ımensions, metres (feet): 111.6 × 12.8 × 4.3
6 × 42 × 14)
craft: 1 × CH-124 Sea King ASW helicopter
ıns: 1 × 2 76 mm forward
'pedoes: 2 × 3 324 mm Mk 32 tubes for Mk 46
W LWT
W Weapons: 1 × 3 Limbo Mk 10 mortar (except
H233)
nar: (DDH233 only) SQR 501 ETASS low-frequency
ed array, SQS 503 hull-mounted medium-frequency
ive, SQS 504 variable depth medium-frequency
've, SQS 502 hull-mounted high-frequency active
ack, SQS 501 hull-mounted high-frequency target
ssification
dar: SPS 12 D band air search, SPS 10 G band
face search, SPG 48 I/J band fire control, Sperry Mk
band navigation
ion Information Organisation: ADLIPS
ıchinery: 2 × English Electric geared turbines,
,000 hp, 2 × shafts, 2 × Babcock & Wilcox boilers
eed, knots: 28
nge, nautical miles: 30
mplement: 233

the immediate post-war period Canada chose to
sign its own First Rate high speed anti-submarine
ıates as a distinctive national type of 'destroyer
ort'. British-designed machinery was employed but
Canadian naval architects German and Milne under
direction of British Naval Constructor Rowland Baker

used Canadian and American equipment and were told to
make the ships look different from the contemporary
British Type 12 frigates. The seven ships were originally
armed with two Mk 10 ASW mortars aft and and twin 76
mm dual-purpose guns fore and aft. All were
modernised in the early 1960s to carry large Sea King
ASW helicopters. The addition of the hangar and flight
deck caused the deletion of one pair of 76-mm guns and
one set of mortars. The original funnel was replaced by
two parallel stacks ahead of the hangar. The ships
underwent DELEX (Destroyer Life Extension Program)
modernisation between 1980 and 1985. *Fraser* was
chosen as a towed array trials ship and an experimental
ETASS system was fitted in a 1986-88 refit. This

installation is being retained. *St Laurent* was laid up in
1974 and sold in 1979 and the survivors now also being
withdrawn from service due to their age. *Assiniboine* has
already been paid off. *Saguenay* and *Margaree* were built
by Halifax Shipyards and were launched in 1953 and
1956. *Skeena* was built by Burrard Dry Dock and
Shipbuilding, *Vancouver* and was launched in August
1952. *Ottawa* was built by Canadian Vickers of Montreal,
launched in in April 1953 and *Fraser* was built by Yarrow
of Esquimault and launched in February 1953.

Photograph: *Fraser* (HM Steele)

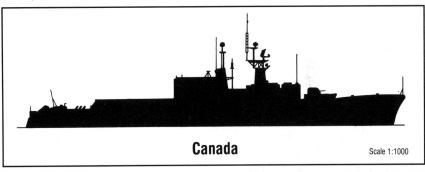

Canada

Scale 1:1000

Number in class: 4

GATINEAU DD236 1959 A
RESTIGOUCHE DD257 1958 P
KOOTENAY DD258 1959 P
TERRA NOVA DD259 1959 P

Destroyers (DD)
Improved Restigouche Class

ecifications
d Technical Data

placement, tonnes: 2,900
ensions, metres (feet): 113.1 × 12.8 × 4.3
1 × 42 × 14.1)
siles: ASW: 1 × 8 ASROC, 16 missiles
s: 1 × 2 76 mm forward
pedoes: 2 × 3 324 mm Mk 32 tubes for
46 ASW LWT
ar: SQS 505 hull-mounted and variable depth
dium-frequency, SQS 501 high-frequency
-mounted target classification
ar: SPS 503 E/F band air search, SPS 10 G band
ace search, Decca 127E I band navigation,
48 I/J band fire control
on Information Organisation: ADLIPS
:hinery: 2 × English Electric geared turbines,
00 hp, 2 × shafts, 2 × boilers
ed, knots: 28
ge, nautical miles: 4,750 at 14 knots
plement: 214

'Restigouche' class was the second batch of
adian destroyer escorts laid down between 1952
1954 and commissioned in 1958-59. Unlike their
ecessors they were armed with the British
3-inch mounting forward. Beginning in 1966 four
e converted to carry the American ASROC missile
em aft in place of the after guns and one of the
nal Limbo mortars. They were also fitted with
able depth sonar and prominent lattice masts.
a Nova completed this process in 1968, Gatineau
972 and the other two in 1973. The three other ships

of the class, *Chaudiere*, *St. Croix* and *Columbia*, were
placed in reserve in 1974. *Columbia* survives as a
harbour training ship at Esquimault. The other two have
been scrapped. The four ASROC ships underwent DELEX
(Destroyer Life Extension Program) modernisation in
1983-86 when they received new radar,
communications, fire control and EW equipment. They
now carry four SRBOC Mk 36 chaff launchers, CANEWS
ESM and the ULQ 36 jammer. They were also fitted with
the ADLIPS action information system. *Gatineau* was
built by Davie of Lauzon, being laid down in April 1953
and launched in June 1957. *Restigouche* was built by
Canadian Vickers of Montreal, being laid down in July
1953 and launched in November 1954. *Kootenay* was

built by Burrard Dry Dock and Shipbuilding of
Vancouver, being laid down in August 1952 and
launched in June 1954. *Terra Nova* was built by the
Victoria Machinery Co., being laid down in November
1952 and launched in June 1955. *Gatineau* was
transferred to the Atlantic in July 1987.

Photograph: *Kootenay* (HM Steele)

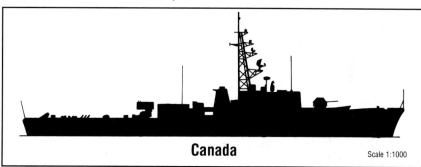

Canada

Scale 1:1000

Number in class: 4

MACKENZIE DD261 1962 P
SASKATCHEWAN DD262 1963 P
YUKON DD263 1963 P
QU'APPELLE DD264 1963 P

Destroyers (DD)
Mackenzie Class

ecifications
d Technical Data

lacement, tonnes: 2,890 full load
ensions, metres (feet): 111.6 × 12.8 × 4.1
× 42 × 14.1)
s: 2 × 2 76 mm, one forward one aft
edoes: 2 × 3 324 mm Mk 32 tubes for
46 ASW LWT
W Weapons: 2 × 3 Limbo Mk 10 mortars
ar: SQS 505 medium-frequency hull-mounted and
able depth, SQS 501 high-frequency hull-mounted
et classification
ar: SPS 12 D band air search, SPS 10 G band
ace search, SPG 48 and SPG 34 I/J band fire control
on Information Organisation: ADLIPS
hinery: 2 × English Electric geared turbines,
00 hp, 2 × shafts, 2 × Babcock and Wilcox
ers
ed, knots: 28
ge, nautical miles: 4,750 at 14 knots
plement: 210

se ships are the only 'St. Laurent' series destroyer
rts to remain in service in their original condition.
y were the third batch completed with modifications
eir accommodation, pre-wetting NBCD
ngements and bridge and upper deck fittings to cope
arctic conditions. All but *Qu'Appelle* carry two
nct types of 3-inch gun. The forward mounting in
other three ships is a British Mk 6 with two 70 calibre
els capable of over 100 rounds per minute per gun.
imum range is 19,500 yards and muzzle velocity is
0 feet per second. The after mounting (both

mountings in *Qu'Appelle*) is the American 50 calibre
Mk 34. This fires only 45 rounds per minute per barrel
with a range of 14,600 yards and a muzzle velocity of
2,700 feet per second. The different weapons have
separate fire control equipment. These ships received
relatively austere DELEX (Destroyer Life Extension
Program) refits carried out at Esquimault by Burrard
between 1982 and 1987. This involved the fitting of new
SQS 505 sonar instead of the previous SQS 503. New
navigational radar, ADLIPS action information
organisation, data links and a torpedo decoy. These
ships, however still lack modern electronic counter-
measures as well as ASW systems and are, therefore,
due for early withdrawal from service by 1993.

Photograph: *Mackenzie* (HM Steele)

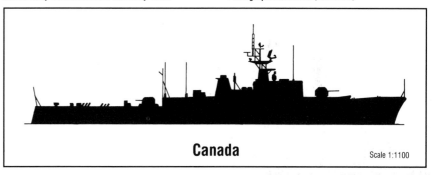

Canada

Scale 1:1100

9

HALIFAX FFH330 1990
VANCOUVER FFH331 1990
VILLE DE QUEBEC FFH332 1990
TORONTO FFH333 1991
REGINA FFH334 1991
CALGARY FFH335 1992
MONTREAL FFH336 1992

FREDERICTON FFH337 1993
WINIPEG FFH338 1994
CHARLOTTETOWN FFH339 1995
ST. JOHN'S FFH340 1995
OTTAWA FFH341 1996

pecifications
ad Technical Data

placement, tonnes: 4,255 full load
ensions, metres (feet): 134.1 × 16.4 × 4.6
0 × 53.8 × 15.1)
raft: 1 × CH 124A Sea King ASW helicopter
siles: SSM: 2 × 4 Harpoon amidships abaft funnel
M: 2 × 8 Sea Sparrow vertical launch system
dships ahead of funnel, 28 missiles
s: 1 × 57 mm forward, 1 × 20 mm Vulcan Phalanx
S aft
edoes: 2 × 2 324 mm Mk 32 tubes for
6 ASW LWT
ar: SQR 501 CANTASS towed array, SQS 505 hull-
nted medium-frequency active
ar: SPS 49(V) C/D long-range air search, Sea Giraffe
0 G band medium range air/surface search, VM 25
K/I/J band fire control, Mk 340 I band navigation
on Information Organisation: SHINPADS
hinery: 2 × General Electric LM 2500 gas turbines,
00 hp, 1 × SEMT-Pielstick 20 PA6-20 8,000 hp
ed, knots: 29
ge, nautical miles: 4,500 at 20 knots on gas
nes, 7,100 at 15 knots on diesels
plement: 225

ss of new Canadian helicopter 'patrol frigates' was
unced at the end of 1977, but the first six were not
red until mid-1983, St John Shipbuilding of New
swick winning the order, in co-operation with
max Electronics of Montreal, an associate of
y(US). A second group of six was announced in
984 and was ordered at the end of 1987. *Halifax*

was laid down in March 1987 and launched in May 1988
at the St. John Yard, and *Vancouver* and *Toronto* were
laid down in February 1988 and launched in February
1989. Half the class was sub-contracted to Marine
Industries, Sorel where *Ville de Québec* was laid down in
December 1988 and *Regina* in October 1989. *Calgary* is
also to be built at Sorel, but the entire second batch will
be built by St. John. The programme was delayed in the
mid-1980s by steel problems. The ships are primarily
anti-submarine vessels and will replace the old destroyer
escorts to form the backbone of the Canadian Navy in the
next century. The design has the potential to be
expanded to improve both its accommodation and air
defence capability. A full EW fit is planned with Shield

chaff and flare rocket launchers, CANEWS ESM and the
Ramses jammer. An SLQ 25 torpedo decoy system will
also be carried along with a bubbler noise signature
reduction system. The CANTASS towed array system
combines a Canadian-made Computing Devices signal
processor with an American SQR 19 'wet end'. The
normal peacetime complement will be 185. It is planned
to replace the Sea King helicopter by the EH-101 Merlin.

Illustration: Artist's impression of 'Halifax' class
(Naval Forces)

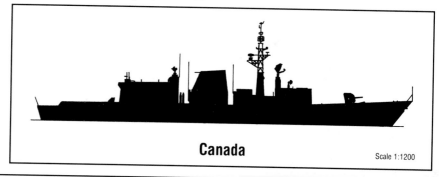

Canada

Scale 1:1200

Number in class: 3

OGIBWA SS72 1965 A
ONONDAGA SS73 1967 A
OKANAGAN SS74 1968 A

Submarines (SS)
Oberon Class

ecifications
d Technical Data

placement, tonnes: 2,410 submerged
ensions, metres (feet): 90 × 8.1 × 5.5
5.2 × 26.5 × 18)
pedo tubes: 6 × 533 mm forward, 2 × 533 mm aft
ar: Krupp-Atlas CSU 3-41 medium-frequency active/
sive, 2007 low-frequency long-range passive flank
y, BQG 501 Sperry Micropuffs passive ranging
ar: 1006 I band navigation
on Information Organisation: Singer Librascope
S
chinery: 2 × Admiralty 16VMS diesels, 3,280 hp,
electric motors, 6,000 hp, 2 × shafts
ed, knots: 12 surfaced, 17 submerged
nplement: 65

ada decided in 1962 to purchase three submarines to
ace the Royal Navy boats previously based there.
y were of the latest British 'Oberon' type and the first
been laid down at Chatham Dockyard that year as
S *Onyx*. She was transferred, renamed and launched
ebruary 1964. Her two sisters were built in the same
e, being launched in September 1965 and
tember 1966. Certain changes were made to meet
adian requirements both in communications
pment and air conditioning capacity. They were
inally fitted with the standard British Type 187
-mounted active/passive sonar but this was replaced
he current German system under SOUP (Submarine
rational Update Project). The submarines completed

their updates in 1982, 1984 and 1986. The new active
transducer was placed in the fin with passive transducer
in the bow dome. A new fire control system, which
utilises a Sperry UYK-20 computer, was fitted. The boats
are being upgraded by Singer Librascope to use the Mk
48 dual-purpose heavyweight torpedo. The after tubes
still fire the short NT37C anti-submarine torpedo. It was
originally intended to replace these submarines with four
new conventional boats but this plan was changed to a
proposal to procure 10-12 nuclear-powered submarines
from either the United Kingdom or France. This
ambitious project was cancelled in 1989 on grounds of
cost and various conventional/air independent
propulsion alternatives are currently being considered.

In the meantime the 'Oberons' are being further
upgraded with the British Triton (2051) integrated sonar
system, including towed array.

Photograph: *Onondaga* (HM Steele)

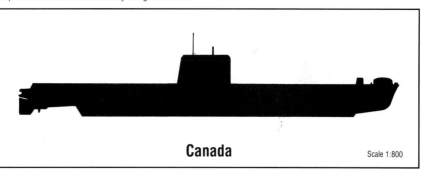

Canada

Scale 1:800

OHIO SSBN726 1981 P
MICHIGAN SSBN727 1982 P
FLORIDA SSBN728 1983 P
GEORGIA SSBN729 1984 P
HENRY M. JACKSON SSBN730 1984 P
ALABAMA SSBN731 1985 P

ALASKA SSBN732 1986 P
NEVADA SSBN733 1986 P
TENNESSEE SSBN734 1988 A
PENNSYLVANIA SSBN735 1989
WEST VIRGINIA SSBN736 1990
KENTUCKY SSBN737 1990
MARYLAND SSBN738 1991

NEBRASKA SSBN739 1992
SSBN740 1994
SSBN741 1994
SSBN742 1995
SSBN743 1996
SSBN744 1997
SSBN745 1998

SSBN746 1999
SSBN747
SSBN748
SSBN749

Displacement, tonnes: 19,050 submerged
Dimensions, metres (feet): 170.7 × 12.8 × 10.8 (560 × 42 × 35.5)
Missiles: (SSBN 726-733) 24 × Trident C-4 (SSBN 734 onwards) Trident II D-5 ballistic missiles
Torpedo tubes: 4 × 533 mm forward
Sonar: BQQ 6 integrated passive search system with BQS 13 spherical bow array and BQR 15 passive towed array, also two passive flank arrays and BQS 15 active/passive high-frequency under-ice and mine avoidance; BQR 19 high-frequency active mast mounted navigation
Radar: BPS 15 I/J band surface search, navigation and fire control
Machinery: 1 × General Electric S8G pressurised water-cooled reactor, 2 × geared turbines, 60,000 hp, 1 × shaft
Speed, knots: about 30
Range, nautical miles: normal endurance 70 days
Complement: up to 184 (authorised complement 156)

The first new submarine for the Trident SLBM system was funded in Fiscal 1974 with ten boats to be built by 1982; delays were caused by design changes and project management and shipyard problems. The first nine were equipped with the Trident C-4 missile, 10.4 metres long with a range of 4,350 nautical miles. Each missile covers eight multiple independently targeted re-entry vehicles (MIRVs), each with a yield of 100 kt. Reported circular error probability is 1,500 feet, with stellar inertial update guidance. The 'Ohio' class were, however, built to take the 13.9 metre D-5 Trident II

missile. This can carry up to eight 475 kt MIRVs over 6,000 nautical miles with a CEP of only 300 feet. It began tests in SSBN734 in 1989 and goes to sea operationally in 1990. SSBN726-733 are based at Bangor, Washington; the D-5 armed boats will be based at King's Bay, Georgia. It is planned to give each boat a 25-day refit after each 70 day patrol. The boat will then go to sea with its second crew. Submarines will have a year-long refit every nine years. The class has been built by the Electric Boat Division of General Dynamics at Groton, Connecticut. Newport News Shipbuilding are also tendering for these submarines. Unit costs of each vessel are about $1,500-1,600 million. Reported operating depth is over 300 metres. The USN still hopes

for 24 'Ohios', but 20 may be the more likely total. It is uncertain whether the C-4 boats will be refitted with D-5 or be replaced by a new 16-tube SSBN design.

Photograph: *Ohio* 1982 (USNI)

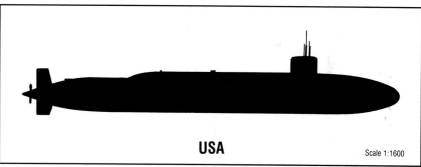

USA

Scale 1:1600

Number in class: 13 and 12

Lafayette Class
LAFAYETTE SSBN616 1963 A
ALEXANDER HAMILTON SSBN617
    1963 A
JOHN ADAMS SSBN620 1964 A
WOODROW WILSON SSBN624
    1963 A
HENRY CLAY SSBN625 1964 A

DANIEL WEBSTER SSBN626
    1964 A
JAMES MADISON SSBN627 1964 A
TECUMSEH SSBN628 1964 A
DANIEL BOONE SSBN629 1964 A
JOHN C. CALHOUN SSBN630 1964 A
ULYSSES S. GRANT SSBN631
    1964 A

N STEUBEN SSBN632 1964 A
SIMIR PULASKI SSBN633 1964 A
ONEWALL JACKSON SSBN634 1964 A

Benjamin Franklin Class
BENJAMIN FRANKLIN SSBN640 1965 A
SIMON BOLIVAR SSBN641 1965 A
KAMEHAMEHA SSBN642 1965 A
GEORGE BANCROFT SSBN643 1966 A
LEWIS AND CLARK SSBN644 1965 A
JAMES K. POLK SSBN645 1966 A
GEORGE C. MARSHALL SSBN654 1966 A

HENRY L. STIMSON SSBN655 1966 A
GEORGE WASHINGTON CARVER SSBN656 1966 A
FRANCIS SCOTT KEY SSBN657 1966 A
MARIANO G. VALLEJO SSBN658 1966 A
WILL ROGERS SSBN659 1967 A

splacement, tonnes: 8,382 submerged
mensions, metres (feet): 129.5 × 10.1 × 9.6 25 × 33 × 31.5)
ssiles: (SSBN616-7/20/24-28/31/42/44-5/54/56/59) × Poseidon C-3 ballistic missiles; (rest) 16 × Trident 4 ballistic missiles
rpedo tubes: 4 × 533 mm forward
nar: BQR 7 passive search, BQR 15 passive low-quency towed array, BQR 19 high-frequency active vigation, BQR 21 hull-mounted passive detection and cking hull array, BQS 4 active search and ssification
dar: BPS 11A or BPS 15 I/J band surface search
achinery: 1 × Westinghouse S5W pressurised water actor, 2 × geared turbines, 15,000 hp, 1 × shaft
eed, knots: 25
nge, nautical miles: normal endurance 70 days
mplement: 143

e main production version of the Polaris submarine ocured in quantity in two batches in the mid-1960s. e second batch of twelve boats, the 'Benjamin anklins', have quieter machinery. Both classes were itted between 1970 and 1978 to carry the Poseidon ssile. This 10.4 metre weapon carries ten 50 kt MIRVs er 3,200 nautical miles. In 1978 conversion of twelve bmarines to carry the Trident C-4 missile began. This s completed at the end of 1982. The first Trident bmarine was SSBN657 which made its first ployment in October 1979. Trident submarines erate from King's Bay, Georgia with Poseidon boats

home-ported at New London, Connecticut and Charleston, South Carolina. They use Holy Loch, UK as a forward base. Six Poseidon 'Lafayettes' have already been decommissioned to keep US SLBM numbers within the limits of the SALT Treaty.; *Sam Rayburn* (1985), *Nathan Hale* and *Nathaniel Green* (1986), *Andrew Jackson* (1988) and *James Monroe* and *Henry Clay* (1989). SSBN635 is used as a dockside training facility, the others are stored in reserve with their missile tubes deactivated. All Poseidon boats will have gone by 1998. Builders were the Electric Boat Division of General Dynamics (SSBN616-7,623/6/8/31/33/40/43/45/55/57/59), Portsmouth Naval Shipyard (SSBN620/36), Newport News Shipbuilding (SSBN622/5/7/30/32/35/41/

44/54/56) and Mare Island Naval Shipyard (SSBN619/24/9/34/42/58). Like the 'Ohios' these submarines carry Mk 48 wire-guided heavyweight torpedoes for self defence. Their patrol cycle is similar to that of the 'Ohios' but they require a refit of almost two years every six years.

Photograph: *Mariano G. Vallejo* (G Arro/USNI)

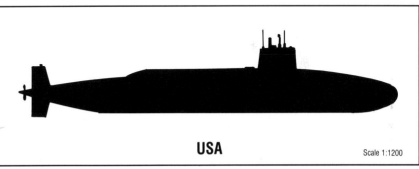

USA

Scale 1:1200

Number in class: Up to 30

SEAWOLF SSN 21 or 774 1995
SSN 1995
SSN 1996
SSN 1997
SSN 1997
(plus 25)

pecifications
nd Technical Data

splacement, tonnes: 9,296 submerged
mensions, metres (feet): 99.4 × 12.9 × 10.9
26.1 × 42.3 × 35.8)
rpedo tubes: 8 × 762 mm amidships
nar: BQQ 5 active/passive suite with bow, hull and
wed arrays
dar: BPS I/J band surface search navigation and fire
ntrol
tion Information Organisation: BSY-2(V)
achinery: 1 × General Electric S6W 60,000 hp,
× shaft pumpjet
eed, knots: 35
nge, nautical miles: limited only by endurance of
w
mplement: 130

own as the SSN21 (meaning a submarine for the 21st
ntury rather than a pennant number) this new type of
bmarine was first projected in 1982. The design
aces great emphasis on quiet operation with an
ended silent speed of 20 knots, achieved with the
ctor operating on natural circulation only. The boats
l have a smaller length to beam ratio than previous
Ns in order to improve manoeuvrability. The diving
nes will be retractable and carried on the hull to
ilitate under-ice operations. In addition the weapons
d has been increased with up to 50 missiles and
pedoes, including the Tomahawk cruise missile and
Mk 48 ADCAP advanced heavyweight torpedo. All
s is achieved at a price with the lead boat costed at
out $2 billion and production boats over $1 billion.

The first SSN21 was laid down at the Electric Boat
Division of General Dynamics in 1989 and two more
have been requested for the Fiscal 1991 programme.
The first of these will be built at Newport News. This
class has been highly controversial, but its major selling
point is the longer time between reactor refuellings
which will significantly reduce through-life costs. Actual
displacement will be about 9,500 tonnes as the flooded
bow sonar dome is considered to be open to the sea and
is not included in the official figure. The pumpjet
propulsion system was pioneered by the British in their
'Trafalgar' class submarines. The 'Seawolf' class will be
highly specialised anti-submarine weapons designed to
have a major acoustic advantage once more over their

Soviet opponents. At the time of writing it was not clear
what the pennant number of this class would be. Even its
name had not been finally decided.

Illustration: Artist's impression of Seawolf
(US Navy/USNI)

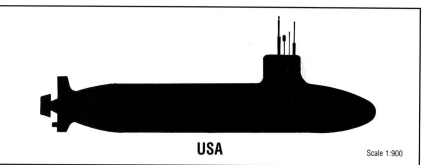

USA

Scale 1:900

Number in class: 62

LOS ANGELES SSN688 1976 P
BATON ROUGE SSN689 1977 A
PHILADELPHIA SSN690 1977 A
MEMPHIS SSN691 1977 A
OMAHA SSN692 1978 P
CINCINNATI SSN693 1978 A
GROTON SSN694 1978 A
BIRMINGHAM SSN695 1978 A
NEW YORK CITY SSN696 1979 P

INDIANAPOLIS SSN697 1980 P
BREMERTON SSN698 1981 P
JACKSONVILLE SSN699
    1981 A
DALLAS SSN700 1981 A
LA JOLLA SSN701 1981 P
PHOENIX SSN702 1981 A
BOSTON SSN703 1982 A
BALTIMORE SSN704 1982 A

CITY OF CORPUS CHRISTI
    SSN705 1983 A
ALBUQUERQUE SSN706 1983 A
PORTSMOUTH SSN707 1983 A
MINNEAPOLIS-SAINT PAUL
    SSN708 1984 A
HYMAN G. RICKOVER SSN709
    1984 A
AUGUSTA SSN710 1985 A

SAN FRANCISCO SSN711 1981 P
ATLANTA SSN712 1982 A
HOUSTON SSN713 1982 P
NORFOLK SSN714 1983 A
BUFFALO SSN715 1983 A
SALT LAKE CITY SSN716 1984 A
OLYMPIA SSN717 1984 P
HONOLULU SSN718 1985 P
PROVIDENCE SSN719 1985 A

TSBURGH SSN720 1985 A
CAGO SSN721 1986 P
Y WEST SSN722 1987 A
LAHOMA CITY SSN723 1988 A
UISVILLE SSN724 1986 A
LENA SSN725 1987 P
WPORT NEWS SSN750 1989 A
N JUAN SSN751 1988 A
SADENA SSN752 1989 P

ALBANY SSN753 1989
TOPEKA SSN754 1989
MIAMI SSN755 1989
SCRANTON SSN756 1990
ALEXANDRIA SSN757 1990
ASHEVILLE SSN758 1990
JEFFERSON CITY SSN759 1991
ANNAPOLIS SSN760 1991
SPRINGFIELD SSN761 1992

COLUMBUS SSN762 1992
SANTA FE SSN763 1992
BOISE SSN764 1991
MONTPELIER SSN765 1992
CHARLOTTE SSN766 1992
HAMPTON SSN767 1992
HARTFORD SSN768
TOLEDO SSN769
TUCSON SSN770

COLUMBIA SSN771
GREENEVILLE SSN772
SSN773

splacement, tonnes: 7,038 submerged
mensions, metres (feet): 109.7 × 10.1 × 9.9
50 × 33 × 32)
ssiles: (SSN719 onwards) 12 vertical launch tubes for
mahawk SLCM forward
rpedo tubes: 4 × 533 mm amidships
nar: BQQ 5A(V)1 or BQQ 5D low-frequency active/
ssive search and attack, BQR 23/25 low-frequency
ssive towed array, BQS 15 high-frequency active
der-ice and mine avoidance. (SSN751 onwards have
I MIDAS-mine and ice detection avoidance system)
dar: BPS 15A I/J band surface search navigation and
e control
tion Information Organisation: (SSN751 onwards)
Y-1
achinery: 1 × General Electric S6G pressurised
ter-cooled reactor, 35,000 hp, 1 × shaft
eed, knots: 30 plus
nge, nautical miles: limited only by endurance of
ew
mplement: 133

gh speed attack submarines built both to counter the
viet 'Victor' class submarines and to operate with fast
rier battle groups. There are effectively four separate
tches; SSN688-699 which were originally fitted with
alogue Mk 113 fire control systems; SSN700-718
uipped with the digital Mk 117 fire control system;
N719-25/750, the first 'improved' models with
rtical launched tubes for Tomahawk cruise missiles
d SSN751 onwards fully modified for under-ice

operations with hull-mounted diving planes and the
BSY-1 integrated combat system. The Mk 117 digital fire
control system is being fitted into earlier boats. 26
weapons are carried for the torpedo tubes, 14 Mk 48
torpedoes, 4 Sub-Harpoon anti-ship missiles and 8
Tomahawk cruise missiles (the Tomahawk can only be
used by submarines fitted with digital fire control). Some
of these submarines also carried the SUBROC nuclear
anti-submarine rocket, now being withdrawn from
service. SSN756 onwards are being fitted for mine
laying. It was originally planned to build three more of
these submarines in Fiscal 1991-2 and cancellation of
SSN773-4 was also suggested; SSN773 was finally
ordered alone in November 1989. Reported diving depth
is 450 metres and the S6G reactor lasts 10 or more years
between refuellings. The boats carry a Fairbanks Morse
diesel generator set for emergency propulsion. SSN691
is used as a non-operational research submarine.
Builders are: Newport News (SSN688-9/91/93/95 711-8/
21-23/50/53/6/8-9/64-67/69-70/72-3) and the Electric
Boat Division of General Dynamics.

Photograph: *New York City* (General Dynamics/USNI)

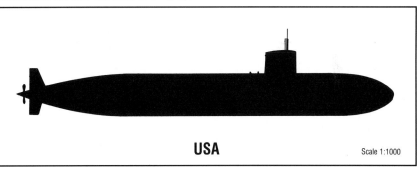

USA

Scale 1:1000

Number in class: 37

STURGEON SSN637 1967 A
WHALE SSN638 1968 A
TAUTOG SSN639 1968 P
GRAYLING SSN646 1969 A
POGY SSN647 1971 P
ASPRO SSN648 1969 P
SUNFISH SSN649 1969 A
PARGO SSN650 1968 A

QUEENFISH SSN651 1966 P
PUFFER SSN652 1969 P
RAY SSN653 1967 A
SAND LANCE SSN660 1971 A
LAPON SSN661 1967 A
GURNARD SSN662 1968 P
HAMMERHEAD SSN663 1968 A
SEA DEVIL SSN664 1969 A

ARRO SSN665 1972 P
KBILL SSN666 1971 P
GALL SSN667 1969 A
DEFISH SSN668 1969 A
HORSE SSN669 1969 A
ACK SSN670 1970 A
ADO SSN672 1971 P
NG FISH SSN673 1970 A

TREPANG SSN674 1970 A
BLUEFISH SSN675 1971 A
BILLFISH SSN676 1971 A
DRUM SSN677 1972 P
ARCHERFISH SSN678 1971 A
SILVERSIDES SSN679 1972 A
WILLIAM H. BATES SSN680 1973 P
BATFISH SSN681 1972 A

TUNNY SSN682 1974 P
PARCHE SSN683 1974 P
CAVALLA SSN684 1973 P
L. MENDEL RIVERS SSN686
   1975 A
RICHARD B. RUSSELL SSN687
   1975 P

lacement, tonnes: 4,857, (SSN678-687) 5,040
merged
ensions, metres (feet): 89, (SSN678-687)
$\times$ 9.65 $\times$ 8.8 (292, (302.2) $\times$ 31.8 $\times$ 28.9)
edo tubes: 4 $\times$ 533 mm amidships
ar: BQQ 2 or 5 low-frequency active/passive search
attack, BQS 23/25 low-frequency passive towed
y, BQS 8 or BQS 14 high-frequency ice and mine
ction
ar: BPS 14 or BPS 15 I/J band surface search
gation and fire control
hinery: 1 $\times$ Westinghouse S5W pressurised water
tor, 2 $\times$ geared turbines, 15,000 hp, 1 $\times$ shaft
ed, knots: 30
ge, nautical miles: limited only by endurance of
y
plement: 107

velopment of the earlier 'Permit' class, these boats
e larger sail/fin structures to allow greater room for
ts and navigational sonar. The taller fin and low
roplanes also allow better control and depth-keeping
e to the surface. The 'Sturgeon' class are very
able for Arctic operations and their diving planes can
otated vertically to facilitate breaking through ice.
y also have strengthened sail and rudder caps. Up to
veapons are carried, a mix of Mk 48 torpedoes,
oon missiles and Tomahawk missiles. These boats
e also fitted to carry the obsolete SUBROC nuclear
oon. The 'Sturgeons' were originally fitted with
113 analogue fire control systems which are being

replaced by the Mk 117 digital systems. The later boats
were lengthened to facilitate fitting BQQ 5 sonar. In 1982
Cavalla was converted to carry a swimmer delivery
vehicle in the amphibious role. SSN678/9, 682 and 686
are also being converted to this role. SSN666, 672, 680
and 687 have been modified to carry deep submergence
rescue vehicles (DSRV) on the after casing. SSN679 and
687 have an extra housing abaft the sail to contain a new
type of communications buoy. Builders were:
Electric Boat Division of General Dynamics
(SSN637/650/667-9/673-6/678-9/681/684), the Quincy
Division of General Dynamics (SSN638/649),
the Ingalls Shipbuilding Corporation (SSN639/647-8/
652/680/682-3), Newport News Shipbuilding

(SSN651-3/661/663-4/668/670/686-7), Portsmouth
Naval Shipyard (SSN660) and San Francisco Naval
Shipyard (SSN662/665-6/672/677). SSN651 and 664
were slated for early decommissioning in the Fiscal 1991
Budget to save reactor refuelling costs, but it is still
doubtful if this will actually happen.

Photograph: *Puffer* 1981 (USNI)

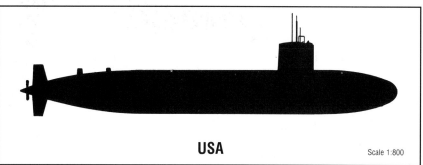

USA

Scale 1:800

pecifications
d Technical Data

placement, tonnes: 5,924 submerged
nensions, metres (feet): 95.9 × 11.5 × 8.2
4.6 × 37.7 × 27)
pedo tubes: 4 × 533 mm amidships
ar: BQQ 5 low-frequency search and attack, BQR 25 -frequency towed array, BQS 8 high-frequency active and mine detection
dar: BPS 14 I/J band surface search navigation and control
chinery: 1 × General Electric S5G pressurised er-cooled reactor, 17,000 hp, 1 × shaft
eed, knots: 25
ige, nautical miles: limited only by endurance of w
nplement: 129

S *Narwhal* was laid down by the Electric Boat Division eneral Dynamics on 17 January 1966, was launched 9 September 1967 and was commissioned on July 1969. She was projected in the Fiscal 1964 gramme to test the S5G natural circulation reactor. s type of reactor is inherently quieter and more able than a normal PWR due to the lack of large lant pumps and their electrical and control ipment. The installation seems to have been a cess in that *Narwhal* remains a fully operational boat, the power and speed disadvantages of the S5G sed pumps to be reintroduced in the S6G of the s Angeles' class for high speed performance. whal was originally fitted with the BQQ 2 sonar tem but this was upgraded to BQQ 5 on refit.

Her Mk 113 analogue fire control system was also replaced by a digitial Mk 117. She carries Mk 48 torpedoes and Sub-Harpoon anti-ship missiles and is being fitted to carry the Tomahawk SLCM. Normal loadings are 4 Harpoons and 8 Tomahawks. In all but her reactor arrangements *Narwhal* is very similar to the contemporary S5W powered 'Sturgeon' class submarines and is, like them, very suitable for under-ice operations. In these her noise advantage at low speed is a significant asset. The other experimental submarine *Glennard P. Lipscomb* (SSN685) with turbo-electric power plant was decommissioned at the beginning of 1990.

Photograph: Narwhal (USNI)

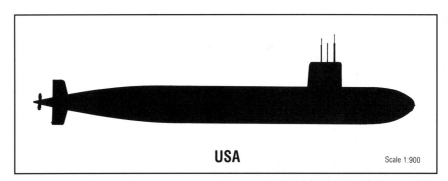

USA

Scale 1:900

Number in class: 8

PERMIT SSN594 1962 P
HADDO SSN604 1964 P
TINOSA SSN606 1964 A
GUARDFISH SSN612 1966 P

FLASHER SSN613 1966 P
GREENLING SSN614 1967 A
GATO SSN615 1968 A
HADDOCK SSN621 1967 P

Nuclear-Powered Attack Submarines (SSN)
Permit Class

pecifications
nd Technical Data

placement, tonnes: 4,349, (SSN613-5) 4,310
merged

nensions, metres (feet): 84.9, (SSN605) 90.6,
N613-5) 89.1 × 9.6 × 8.7 (278.5/297.4/292.2 ×
7 × 28.4)

pedo tubes: 4 × 533 mm amidships

ar: BQQ 2 or 5 active/passive search and attack,
R 23 passive towed array, BQS 14 high-frequency
e and ice detection

lar: BPS 11 or 15 I/J band surface search navigation
fire control

chinery: 1 × Westinghouse S5W pressurised
er-cooled reactor, 2 × geared turbines, 15,000 hp,
shaft

ed, knots: 30

ge, nautical miles: limited only by endurance of
v

mplement: 127

was originally the 'Thresher' class but the name
, USS *Thresher* (SSN593), was lost in the worst
ster in US submarine history during deep diving
s on 10 April 1963. The design was a new one to give
ter depth capability and a high degree of quietness,
ce the significant increase in size over the previous
ojack' class. Maximum diving depth is reportedly
ut 400 metres, although age may prevent this now
g achieved by some boats. SSN613-5 were built to a
ntly improved design with larger sails and heavier
hinery. The 'Permit' class were the first American
marines to have their machinery mounted on a

sound-insulated raft to reduce radiated noise. SSN605
was fitted with two contra-rotating propellers with a
direct drive turbine to improve both power efficiency and
acoustic signature. This is now reportedly removed. The
boats were originally fitted with the Mk 113 fire control
system but this is being replaced in those boats that
have been refitted. The decision has been taken to retire
this class early in order to save refuelling costs. Five
boats, *Plunger* (SSN595), *Barb* (SSN596), *Pollack*
(SSN603), *Jack* (SSN605) and *Dace* (SSN607) have
already been decommissioned. The rest are due to go in
1991. Builders were San Francisco Naval Shipyard
(SSN594), Ingalls Shipbuilding (SSN621), New York
Shipbuilding (SSN604/612), Portsmouth Naval Shipyard

(SSN606) and Electric Boat Division of General
Dynamics (SSN613-5). The boats are armed with Mk 48
torpedoes and Sub-Harpoon anti-ship missiles.

Photograph: *Permit* (USNI)

USA

Scale 1:800

ecifications
d Technical Data

lacement, tonnes: 8,006 submerged
ensions, metres (feet): 125 × 10.1 × 9.8
× 33 × 32)
edo tubes: 4 × 533 mm forward
ar: BQR 7 passive search, BQS 4 active passive
ch/attack, BQR 25 low-frequency passive towed
y, BQR 19 high-frequency close-range active
ar: BPS 15 I/J band surface search navigation and
control
hinery: 1 × Westinghouse S5W pressurised
er-cooled reactor, 2 × General Electric turbines,
00 hp, 1 × shaft
ed, knots: 30 Range, nautical miles, limited only be
urance of crew
plement: (SSN609) 132, (SSN611) 125 plus 67
mandos

se are the surviving boats of the five 'Ethan Allen'
s built about 1960 to carry Polaris missiles. They
ied out their last deterrent patrols in 1981 and when
ctivated under the terms of the SALT Treaty were
verted in 1983-6 as special operations submarines,
sports for SEAL special forces. The submarines can
y up to two Dry Deck Shelters (DDS) to
ommodate the frogmen or a swimmer delivery
cle. The swimmers can enter or leave the DDS while
boat is submerged. The 16 missile tubes are filled
cement ballast and one of the original ship's inertial
gation systems and the Polaris missile control
pment have been removed. SSN609 was laid down
ewport News Shipbuilding on 28 December 1959,

was launched on 2 February 1961 and was
commissioned on 6 March 1962. SSN611 was built at
the same yard and laid down on 4 April 1960, launched
on 15 July 1961 and commissioned on 21 May 1962.
These submarines have also been used to evaluate the
feasibility of submarine deployment of the very
long-range Surveillance Towed Array Sensor System
(SURTASS). The three other boats of the class,
Ethan Allen (SSN608), *Thomas A Edison* (SSN610) and
Thomas Jefferson (SSN618) were all stricken for
scrapping in 1986. Older American SSNs and SSBNs are
all now decommissioned and stricken, the USS *Nautilus*,
the pioneer SSN, having became a museum ship in
1985.

Photograph: *Sam Houston* as SSBN (Edward J O'Brien/
USNI)
Silhouette: *Ethan Allan* with dry-dock shelter

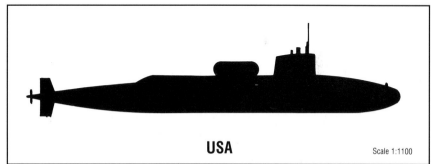

USA

Scale 1:1100

Number in class: 5

THEODORE ROOSEVELT CVN71 1986 A
ABRAHAM LINCOLN CVN72 1989 P
GEORGE WASHINGTON CVN73 1991
JOHN C. STENNIS CVN74 1998
UNITED STATES CVN75 1998

ecifications
d Technical Data

lacement, tonnes: (CVN71) 97,933, (CVN72)
,500 full load
ensions, metres (feet): 332.9 × 40.8 × 11.8
92 × 134 × 38.7)
raft: 86; 20 × F-14 Tomcat fighters, 20 × F/A-18
net fighter/attack, 5 × EA-6B Prowler EW,
× A-6 Intruder all weather attack, 5 × E-2C Hawkeye
V, 10 × S-3A Viking ASW, 6 × SH-3 Sea King ASW
copters
siles: SAM: 3 × 8 Sea Sparrow
s: 4 × 20 mm Vulcan Phalanx CIWS
ar: SPS 48 E/F band 3D air search, SPS 49 C/D band
search, SPS 67V G band surface search, SPN 43, 44,
and 46 J/K/E/F band carrier landing aid, LN 66 I/J
d navigation, SPS 64 I/J band navigation,
57 I/J band fire control
on Information Organisation: NTDS
chinery: 2 × General Electric A4W/A1G pressurised
er-cooled reactors, 4 × geared turbines,
,000 hp, 4 × shafts
ed, knots: 30 plus
urance: 16 days steady flying, 15 years between
tor refuellings
plement: 6,286 including 2,512 air wing

odore Roosevelt was authorised under the Fiscal
) Budget after considerable controversy over the
struction of new CVNs. Alternative smaller designs
been put forward but Congressional pressure forced
adoption of a modified Nimitz design. Secretary of
Navy Lehman pressed for two carriers to be put

simultaneously into the Fiscal 1982 programme. It was
claimed that simultaneous ordering would save money.
Similarly the last two ships were ordered simultaneously
in June 1988. All these ships are constructed by
Newport News Shipbuilding, the only yard capable of
producing them. *Theodore Roosevelt* was laid down on
31 October 1981 and was launched on 27 October 1984.
She was commissioned on 28 October 1986. *Abraham
Lincoln* was laid down on 3 November 1984, launched
on 13 February 1988 and commissioned on 11
December 1989. *George Washington* was laid down in
August 1986 and is due for completion at the end of
1991. *John C Stennis*, named after the former Chairman
of the Senate Armed Services and Appropriations

Committees, is due to be laid down in 1991 and
completed in 1998. The *United States* will be laid down
in 1992 and should also complete in 1998. The flight
deck of these ships is 332.9 metres (1,092 feet) long
and the hangar is 7.8 metres (25.6 feet) high. There are
four steam catapults and the ship can launch an aircraft
every 20 seconds. There are four arrester wires and four
barriers. 9,145 tonnes of aviation fuel is carried and the
magazines hold 1,985 tonnes of aviation ordnance
stores. CVN72, in addition to extra protection, has new
lower pressure catapults. The ships are protected with
2.5-inch steel armour and Kevlar.

Photograph: *Abraham Lincoln* 1989 (USNI)

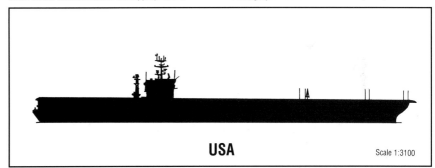

USA

Scale 1:3100

ecifications
d Technical Data

acement, tonnes: 92,955 full load
nsions, metres (feet): 332.9 × 40.8 × 11.3
2 × 134 × 37)
aft: 86; 20 × F-14 Tomcat fighters,
 F/A-18 Hornet fighter/attack, 5 × EA-6B Prowler
20 × A-6 Intruder all weather attack,
E-2C Hawkeye AEW, 10 × S-3A Viking ASW,
SH-3 Sea King ASW helicopters
iles: SAM: 3 × 8 Sea Sparrow
: (CVN68-9) 3, (CVN70) 4 × 20 mm Vulcan
anx CIWS
r: SPS 48 E/F band 3D air search, SPS 49 C/D band
earch, SPS 67V G band surface search, SPN 41, 42,
nd 44 J/K/E/F band carrier landing aid,
64 I/J band navigation, Mk 115 I/J band fire control,
5 D band target acquisition system
n Information Organisation: NTDS
ninery: 2 × General Electric A4W/A1G pressurised
-cooled reactors, 4 × geared turbines,
00 hp, 4 × shafts
d, knots: 30 plus
rance: 16 days steady flying, 13 years between
or refuellings
lement: 6,286 including 2,624 airwing

66 at the height of the Vietnam War, Secretary of
nse McNamara announced the augmentation of the
uclear Carrier Force to four ships with three new
els to be completed in the 1970s. *Nimitz* was laid
n at the Newport News Shipbuilding Yard in June
 and the *Eisenhower* on 15 August 1970.

Controversy delayed laying down the third ship until
October 1975. The three carriers were launched on
13 May 1972, 11 October 1975 (which was also the day
CV70 was laid down) and 15 March 1980. The 'Nimitz'
class differ from the prototype nuclear-powered carrier,
Enterprise, in that they are powered by only two
reactors. With Vietnam experience in mind the ships
were given large aviation fuel and magazine spaces.
There is 15,134 cubic metres (530,450 cubic feet) of
magazine space which can hold 1,985 tonnes of aviation
ordnance. The total payload that is associated with the
air group is about 15,250 tonnes. These ships were
some of the only armoured vessels of their period with
protected hulls and decks and considerable internal

subdivision. It is estimated that ships of this class are
capable of withstanding three times the damage of a
World War II 'Essex' class ship. Extra protection is being
fitted on refit. CVN70 was completed with an
anti-submarine control centre reflecting the broadening
of the attack carrier (CVA) role to include ASW. This
facility will be retro-fitted to her sisters. The official
designation of the first two ships was changed from
CVAN to CVN on 30 June 1975.

Photograph: *Nimitz* 1981 (USNI)

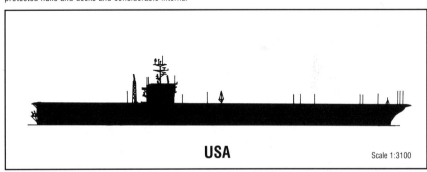

USA

Scale 1:3100

●ecifications
▮d Technical Data

▮lacement, tonnes: 92,430 full load
▮ensions, metres (feet): 331.6 × 40.5 × 11.9
▮88 × 133 × 39)
▮raft: 86; 20 × F-14 Tomcat fighters,
▮× F/A-18 Hornet fighter/attack, 5 × EA-6B Prowler
▮:ronic warfare, 20 × A-6 all weather attack,
▮ E-2C Hawkeye AEW, 10 × S-3A Viking ASW,
▮ SH-3 Sea King ASW helicopters
▮siles: SAM: 3 × 8 Sea Sparrow
▮s: 3 × 20 mm Vulcan Phalanx CIWS
▮ar: SPS 48 3D E/F band air search, SPS 49 C/D band
▮earch, SPS 65 D band air search, SPS 67 G band
▮ace search, SPN 35A, 41, 42 and 44 J/K/E/F band
▮er landing aid, SPS 64 I/J band navigation,
▮91 fire control, M 25 D band target acquisition
▮em
▮on Information Organisation: NTDS
▮hinery: 8 × Westinghouse A2W presurised
▮r-cooled reactors, 4 × geared steam turbines,
▮000 hp, 4 × shafts
▮ed, knots: 34
▮urance: 12 days intensive flying, about 8 years
▮ween reactor refuellings
▮plement: 5,562 including 2,627 air wing

▮rprise was laid down on 4 February 1958 at Newport
▮s Shipbuilding yard and was launched on
▮eptember 1960. She was commissioned
▮5 November 1961 and served first in the Atlantic and
▮iterranean and then from 1965 in the Pacific. She
▮ered a major flight deck accident off Vietnam in 1969

carried out the final carrier strikes on Vietnam in 1973 and covered the evacuation from Saigon in 1975. She was based on the Kitty Hawk design but with nuclear power to allow the carrying of 50 percent more aviation fuel, to satisfy more easily the huge power demands of an aircraft carrier, to allow unlimited high speed steaming and to prevent aircraft corrosion from boiler gases. *Enterprise* was completed with an advanced SPS 32/33 phased array radars mounted on distinctive 'bill boards' around her island superstructure. These proved hard to maintain and were replaced during her 1979-82 refuelling and modernisation by a Nimitz-type installation, although the distinctive shape of the superstructure was retained. *Enterprise* is due for

another complex overhaul in the early 1990s. A contract has been signed with Newport News Shipbuilding, but both the projected cost, $1.4 billion, and the time to be taken, 3.5 years, has caused has caused considerable concern in Congress and in an atmosphere of defence cuts will be difficult to justify. *Enterprise* has four C13 Mod 1 catapults, 20,666 square metres (216,000 square feet) of hangar space and 7.62 metres (25 feet) high hangars.

Photograph: *Enterprise* 1989 (USNI)

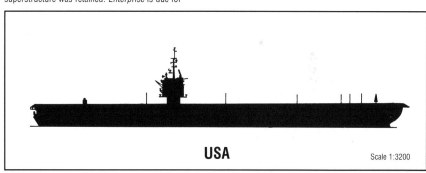

USA

Scale 1:3200

pecifications
nd Technical Data

placement, tonnes: 82,240 full load
nensions, metres (feet): 320.3 × 39.2 × 11.2
)50 × 128.6 × 36.75)
craft: 86; 20 × F-14 Tomcat fighters, 20 × F/A-18
rnet fighter/attack, 5 × EA-6B Prowler EW, 20 × A-6
ruder attack, 5 × E-2C Hawkeye AEW, 10 × S-3A
ing ASW, 6 × SH-3 Sea King ASW helicopters.
ssiles: SAM: 3 × 8 Sea Sparrow
ns: 3 × 20 mm Vulcan Phalanx CIWS
dar: SPS 48C E/F band 3D air search,
S 49 C/D band air search, SPS 67 G band surface
rch, SPN 35, 41, 42 and 43A J/K/E/F band carrier
ding aid, SPN 64 I band navigation, 3 Mk 91 fire
ttrol, Mk 23 D band target acquisition system
ion Information Organisation: NTDS
chinery: 4 × Westinghouse geared turbines,
< Foster Wheeler boilers, 280,000 hp, 4 × shafts
eed, knots: 32
nge, nautical miles: 8,000 at 20 knots
mplement: 5,680 including 2,480 air wing

s was America's last conventionally-powered aircraft
rier, built after considerable controversy over whether
e should be nuclear-propelled. She has a distinctive
erstructure slewed out to starboard to minimise
blems with funnel gases. She was based on the hull
m of USS *America*, but with a new side protective
tem which necessitated considerable internal
rrangement. The flight deck shape was also altered. It
s originally intended to fit her with SQS 23 sonar but
s was deleted as an economy measure. She has four

elevators, two on the starboard side forward and one on
each side abaft the superstructure. There are four
catapults, three 90 metre (295 feet) C 13s and one
94.5 metre (310 feet) C 13-1 catapults. She has an
11,808 square metre (127,104 square feet) aviation
ordnance magazine which can accommodate 1,270
tonnes of ammunition. She carries over 6,000 tonnes of
aviation fuel. *John F. Kennedy* was laid down at the
Newport News Shipbuilding yard on 22 October 1964
and was launched on 27 May 1967. She was
commissioned on 7 September 1968. She is due to
receive a Service Life Extension Program (SLEP) at the
beginning of the next century. She was originally
unarmed and the Sea Sparrow missiles and CIWS gun

systems were added in subsequent refits. She was
originally rated attack carrier (CVA) but was modified to
operate ASW aircraft in 1974 leading to her
redesignation as a multi-mission carrier (CV). CV-67
has always been an Atlantic/Mediterranean ship.

Photograph: *John F. Kennedy* 1988 (William Lipski/
USNI)

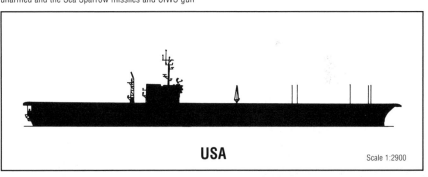

USA

Scale 1:2900

pecifications
ad Technical Data

placement, tonnes: 81,000 full load
nensions, metres (feet): 319.25 × 39.6 × 11.3
147 × 130 × 37)
craft: 86; 20 × F-14 Tomcat fighters, 20 × F/A-18
net attack, 5 × EA-6B Prowler EW,
× A-6 Intruder attack, 5 × E-2C Hawkeye AEW,
× S-3A Viking ASW, 6 × SH-3 Sea King ASW
copters
siles: SAM: 3 × 8 Sea Sparrow
is: 3 × 20 mm Vulcan Phalanx CIWS
lar: SPS 48C E/F band 3D air search,
S 49 C/D band air search, SPS 67 G band surface
rch, SPN 35, 41, 42 and 43A J/K/E/F band carrier
ding aid, SPN 64 I band navigation, 3 Mk 91 fire
trol, Mk 23 D band target acquisition system
on Information Organisation: NTDS
chinery: 4 × Westinghouse geared turbines,
Foster Wheeler boilers, 280,000 hp, 4 × shafts
ed, knots: 32
ge, nautical miles: 8,000 at 20 knots
nplement: 5,433 including 2,480 air group

owing the building of the *Enterprise* it was decided
a conventionally-powered carrier was adequate for
sting requirements given the very high cost of a
AN. After considering a smaller nuclear-powered ship
as decided to build a repeat Kitty Hawk with some
difications. These included a longer C13-1 steam
apult in addition to three more standard C13s.
ship was also fitted with an SQS 23 sonar for self
tection from Soviet SSN attack. Given the

contemporary fear of nuclear attack it was thought the
screen might have to be too dispersed to cope with this
new threat. The sonar was removed in 1981. The
America was originally equipped with two twin launchers
or Terrier long-range surface-to-air missiles but these
were removed during her 1982-84 refit. The ship was the
first American carrier to be fitted with an integrated
Combat Information Centre and ASW control centre. She
was also the first to carry Vulcan Phalanx, this being
fitted in April 1980. Like the 'Kitty Hawks' her four
elevators are mounted three on the starboard side and
one abaft on the port side. This facilitates the
simultaneous landing and take off of aircraft. The ship
can be distinguished from the other later conventionally-

powered carriers by her stepped superstructure and
relatively small smoke stack. She was built by Newport
News Shipbuilding, being laid down on 9 January 1961,
launched on 1 February 1964 and commissioned on
23 January 1965. She has served both in the Atlantic/
Mediterranean and in the Pacific where she participated
in the Vietnam war. She is due to undergo her SLEP
(Service Life Extension Program) in 1996-99

Photograph: *America* (HM Steele)

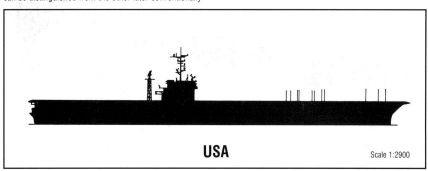

USA

Scale 1:2900

ecifications
d Technical Data

lacement, tonnes: (CV63) 82,425, (CV64) 83,085
oad

ensions, metres (feet): 318.8 × 39.6 × 11.4
46 × 130 × 37)

raft: 86; 20 × F-14 Tomcat fighters, 20 × F/A-18
et fighter/attack, 5 × EA-6B Prowler EW,
× A-6 Intruder all weather attack, 5 × E-2C Hawkeye
, 10 × S-3A Viking ASW, 6 × SH-3 Sea King ASW
opters

siles: 3 × 8 Sea Sparrow

s: 3 × 20 mm Vulcan Phalanx CIWS

ar: SPS 48C E/F band 3D air search,
49 C/D band air search, SPS 67 G band surface
ch, SPN 35, 41, 42 and 43A J/K/E/F band carrier
ing aid, SPN 64 I band navigation, 3 Mk 91 fire
rol, Mk 23 D band target acquisition system, being
ed on SLEP (Service Life Extension Program) to
de SPN 46 in the carrier landing aids and to
titute SPS 48E and SPS 49V air search radars

on Information Organisation: NTDS

hinery: 4 × Westinghouse geared turbines,
Foster Wheeler boilers, 280,000 hp, 4 × shafts

ed, knots: 32

ge, nautical miles: 8,000 at 20 knots

plement: (CV63) 5,253, (CV64) 5,497 including
0 air group

3 was laid down by New York Shipbuilding at
den, New Jersey on 27 December 1956 and
stellation at the New York Naval Shipyard, Brooklyn
4 September 1957. Both suffered shipyard

problems, *Constellation* being delayed by a serious fire
on board and the ships were not launched until 1960,
Kitty Hawk on 21 May and *Constellation* on 8 October.
They were commissioned on 29 April and 21 October
1961. Their design reflected dissatisfaction with the two
previous 'Forrestals'. The superstructure of these ships
was set back much further aft and the lifts were
rearranged to allow simultaneous landing and take off.
They have operated in the Pacific (including Vietnam and
Indian Ocean service) and *Kitty Hawk* is due to be
transferred to Yakosuka to replace *Midway* in 1991 on
completion of her Service Life Extension Program
(SLEP) refit. Originally designated CVA they were
reclassified CV in 1973 (CV63) and 1975 (CV64). They

were originally armed with Terrier long-range surface-to-
air missiles and CV64 retained these until her 1982-84
refit. *Constellation* will undergo her SLEP from October
1990 to November 1993. The ships carry four C13 steam
catapults and have four sets of arrester wires. Their
hangar decks are 225.5 metres (740 feet) long, 30.8
metres (101 feet) wide and 7.6 metres (25 feet) high.
As with all large American carriers only a fraction of the
air group can be housed in the hangar at any one time.
These carriers set the pattern for the deck layout of all
subsequent American CVs.

Photograph: *Kitty Hawk* 1987 (USNI)

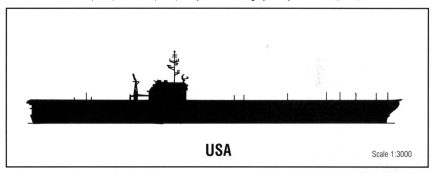

USA

Scale 1:3000

Number in class: 4

FORRESTAL CV59 1955 A
SARATOGA CV60 1956 A
RANGER CV61 1957 P
INDEPENDENCE CV62 1959 A

ecifications
d Technical Data

acement, tonnes: (CV59) 80,522, (CV60) 81,673,
1) 82,466, (CV62) 81,937 full load
nsions, metres (feet): (CV59) 331, (CV60) 324,
1) 326.4, (CV62) 326.1 × 39.6 × 11.3
6/1,063/1,071/1,070 × 130 × 37)
aft: 86; 20 × F-14 Tomcat fighters, 20 × F/A-18
et fighter/attack, 5 × EA-6B Prowler EW, 20 × A-6
der all weather attack, 5 × E-2C AEW, 10 × S-3A
g ASW, 6 × SH-3 Sea King ASW helicopters
les: 3 × 8 Sea Sparrow
: 3 × 20 mm Vulcan Phalanx CIWS
r: SPS 48C E/F band 3D air search,
49 C/D band air search, SPS 67 G band surface
h, SPN 41, 42, 43A and 44 J/K/E/F band carrier
ng aid, SPN 64 I band navigation, 3 Mk 91 fire
ol, Mk 23 D band target acquisition system
n Information Organisation: NTDS
inery: 4 × Westinghouse geared turbines,
3abcock & Wilcox boilers, (CV59) 260,000,
rs) 280,000 hp, 4 × shafts
d, knots: 33
e, nautical miles: 8,000 at 20 knots
lement: (CV59) 5,438, (CV60) 5,376, (CV61)
(CV62) 5,273 including 2,4800 air group.

riginal class of large supercarrier based on the
ve USS *United States* cancelled in April 1949. The
arance of *Forrestal* and *Saratoga* has been more
y altered over the years than their sisters which
the original raked funnels. The class has three lifts
e starboard side, one forward and two abaft the

superstructure and one lift forward on the port side
which interferes with simultaneous landings and take
offs. The *Forrestal* was modified with an angled deck
while under construction. The ships were originally
armed with 5-inch guns and *Ranger* retains the
sponsons. All but *Ranger* have undergone SLEP (Service
Life Extension Program), CV60 in 1980-83, CV59 in
1983-85 and CV62 in 1985-88. CV61 was due to
undergo an incremental maintenance programme, but
may now receive her originally scheduled SLEP in
1993–6. The ships have armoured flight decks and
other protective features from attack above and below
the waterline. CV59 has 615 psi boilers, hence
her reduced power output. The hangar decks are

225.5 metres (740 feet) long, 31 metres (101 feet) wide
and 7.6 metres (25 feet) high. CV59 and CV61 were built
by Newport News Shipbuilding, being laid down in July
1952 and August 1954 and launched in December 1954
and September 1956. CV60 and CV62 were built by New
York Naval Shipyard, being laid down in December 1962
and July 1955 and launched in October 1955 and June
1958. All served off Vietnam although only *Ranger* has
been regularly Pacific deployed.

Photograph: *Independence* (HM Steele)

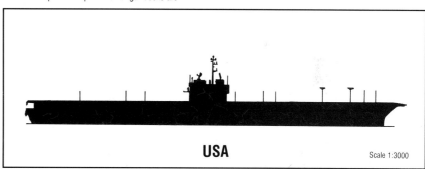

USA

Scale 1:3000

ecifications
d Technical Data

lacement, tonnes: 66,288 full load
ensions, metres (feet): 306 × 36.9 × 10.7
03 × 121 × 35)
aft: 68; 40 × F/A-18 fighter/attack, 12 × A-6 all
er attack, 5 × KA-6 tankers, 3 × E-2C Hawkeye
, 7 × SH-3H Sea King ASW helicopters
s: 3 × 20 mm Vulcan Phalanx CIWS
ar: SPS 48C E/F band 3D air search,
49 C/D band air search, SPS 67 G band surface
ch, SPN 41, 42 and 43A J/K/E/F band carrier landing
SPS 64 I band navigation
n Information Organisation: NTDS
hinery: 4 × Westinghouse geared turbines,
Babcock and Wilcox boilers, 212,000 hp,
shafts
d, knots: 32
e, nautical miles: 15,000 miles at 15 knots
plement: 4,769 including 2,229 air wing

of the three 'Midway' class carriers built in the latter
of the World War II, the first American carriers with
ured flight decks originally designated CVBs. *Coral*
was laid down at Newport News Shipbuilding on
ily 1944, was launched on 2 April 1946 and was
missioned on 1 October 1947. She has been much
fied over the years, her major modernisation taking
between 1957 and 1960. During this rebuild she
red an angled flight deck, strengthened and
ated elevators, three steam catapults and an
sed bow. One elevator is forward and one aft of the
d and there is a portside deck edge elevator on the

quarter. *Coral Sea* served in the Pacific after her
modernisation including Vietnam war operations.
In 1977 she became the training carrier for the Pacific
reserve air groups. In 1979 she returned to first line
service with a deployment to the Indian Ocean. In 1983
she was transferred to Norfolk, Virginia for a refit that
would allow her to remain operational in the Atlantic until
1992-3. She became operational again in 1985. With the
decision in 1989 to reduce to fourteen carrier battle
groups (CVBGs) *Coral Sea* began to deactivate rather
than leave on her planned operational deployment. She
is now due finally to decommission in April 1990. It was
originally intended that she would be replaced by the
George Washington and that she would then become the

Pensacola-based training carrier to replace *Lexington*.
Her fate on decommissioning is now uncertain. *Coral
Sea*'s sister ship *Franklin D Roosevelt* (CV42) was
stricken in 1977.

Photograph: *Coral Sea* 1981 (USNI)

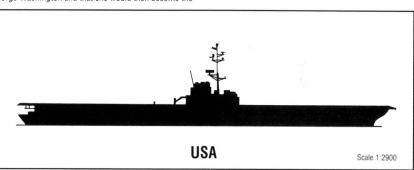

USA

Scale 1:2900

pecifications
d Technical Data

placement, tonnes: 68,583 full load
nensions, metres (feet): 306.9 × 36.9 × 11
06 × 121 × 36)
craft: 62; 36 × F/A-18 fighter/attack,
× A-6 Intruder all weather attack, 4 × EA-6 EW,
E-2C AEW, 6 × SH-3 Sea King ASW helicopters,
siles: SAM: 2 × 8 Sea Sparrow
as: 2 × 20 mm Vulcan Phalanx CIWS
lar: SPS 48C E/F band 3D air search,
49 C/D band air search, SPS 67 G band surface
rch, SPN 35A, 42 and 44 J/K/E/F carrier landing aid,
64 I band navigation, 2 × Mk 115 fire control
ion Information Organisation: NTDS
chinery: 4 × Westinghouse geared turbines,
× Babcock and Wilcox boilers, 212,000 hp,
shafts
ed, knots: 32
ge, nautical miles: 15,000 miles at 15 knots
nplement: 4,680 including 1,854 air wing

way was built by Newport News Shipbuilding, being
down on 27 October 1943 and launched on
March 1945. She was commissioned on
September 1945. Like *Coral Sea,* she received a
or SCB 110 rebuild from 1955 to 1957. In 1966 she
ered San Francisco Naval Shipyard for a further more
nsive \$200 million modernisation coded
101.66. This greatly enlarged her flight deck. She
acquired two new C13 catapults instead of her old
s as retained on *Coral Sea. Midway* was home ported
okosuka, Japan in October 1973. Her superstructure

was extended aft when she was fitted with the SPS 48C
radar in 1979. Her progressive modernisation increased
Midway's draught which made her hangar deck very
wet. In 1986 bulges 183 metres long and 3 metres wide
were added to try to solve the problem. These caused
difficulties of their own, both decreasing the roll period
and increasing flight deck wetness. This forced the ship
to operate with a reduced air group. It was planned to
operate Midway until 1997, but her decommissioning
has now been brought forward to mid-1990 as a result of
the Bush defence review. She will now decommission
when *Abraham Lincoln* joins the Pacific Fleet and be
replaced in Japan by the USS *Ranger* in early 1991. Her
own future is uncertain. *Midway* has operated in the

Pacific since 1955 after initial service in the Atlantic and
Mediterranean. Her hangar is 211 metres (692 feet)
long, 26 metres (85 feet) wide and 5.3 metres
(17.5 feet) high. The 'Midway' class carriers do not
operate fixed wing ASW aircraft or F-14 long-range
interceptors.

Photograph: *Midway* (USNI)

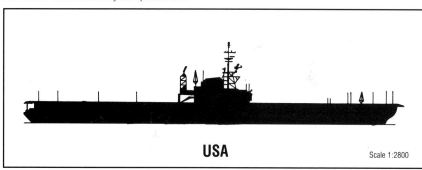

USA

Scale 1:2800

pecifications
nd Technical Data

splacement, tonnes: 43,182 full load
mensions, metres (feet): 272.8 × 31.4 × 9.5
4.5 × 103 × 31)
craft: cannot maintain or support tactical aircraft
dar: SPS 49 C/D band air search, SPS 10 G band
face search, SPS 64 I band navigation
chinery: 4 × Westinghouse geared turbines,
× Babcock and Wilcox boilers, 150,000 hp,
× shafts
eed, knots: 30 plus
nge, nautical miles: 15,000 at 15 knots
mplement: 1,456

e last survivor of the large 'Essex' class that was the
nstay of American carrier force during the Pacific
r, *Lexington* was laid down as the *Cabot* (CV16) at
hlehem Steel, Quincy, Massachussetts on 15 July
41. She was launched on 26 September 1942 and was
mmissioned on 17 February 1943 having been
amed after the carrier lost at the Battle of the Coral
a. She operated throughout the Central Pacific
mpaign participating in both the Battles of the
lippine Sea and Leyte Gulf and being hit by a
mikaze in November 1944. After a period in reserve
m 1947 to 1953 she was modernised into the
ncock' class and recommissioned into the Pacific
et in 1955. In 1963 after a delay caused by the Cuba
sis she became the pilot training ship, home ported at
nsacola, Florida. She was due for withdrawal in 1979

but was retained as her replacement *Coral Sea* was
required as an operational carrier. *Lexington* was due to
be replaced in 1992 by the *Coral Sea* but her future now
depends on the fate of both *Coral Sea* and *Midway* that
are being withdrawn prematurely in 1990. The AVT has
no operational capacity, being unable to maintain or
support aircraft. Four other variously modernised
'Essex' ships, *Bennington* (CVS20), *Bon Homme
Richard* (CV34), *Hornet* (CV12) and *Oriskany* (CV 34)
survived as 'mobilisation assets' in reserve storage at
Bremerton, Washington until the end of the 1980s.
In 1981 *Oriskany* was slated for recommissioning but
this was refused by Congress on grounds of expense
and lack of suitable aircraft. All four are now stricken.

Photograph: *Lexington* (HM Steele)

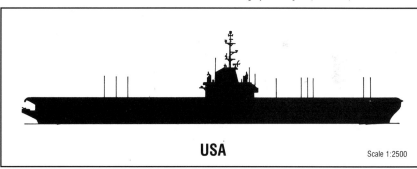

USA

Scale 1:2500

Number in class: 4

IOWA BB61 1943 A
NEW JERSEY BB62 1943 P
MISSOURI BB63 1944 P
WISCONSIN BB64 1944 A

Battleships (BB)
Iowa Class

pecifications
nd Technical Data

splacement, tonnes: 58,274 full load
mensions, metres (feet): 270.4 × 33 × 11.6
37.2 × 108.2 × 38)
craft: helicopter platform aft, up to 5 artillery-spotting
nes
ssiles: SSM: 8 × 4 Tomahawk SLCM amidships,
× 4 Harpoon, two on each side of after funnel
ns: 3 × 3 406 mm, two forward one aft,
× 2 127 mm, three on each beam, 4 × 2 20 mm
*can Phalanx CIWS, two on each beam
dar: SPS 49 C/D band air search, SPS 10 F G/H band
search, SPS 67(V) G band surface search,
S 64 I band navigation, Mk 25, Mk 13 and
G 53F I/ J band fire control
chinery: 4 × (BB61/3) General Electric (BB62/4)
stinghouse geared turbines, 8 × Babcock and Wilcox
lers, 212,000 hp, 4 × shafts
eed, knots: 35
nge, nautical miles: 5,000 at 30 knots,
800 at 20 knots
mplement: 1,518

e last early-20th-century battleships designed in the
1930s as high speed vessels to operate with fast
craft carriers. The main armour belt is 307 mm thick,
ering to 41 mm and 345 mm armour protects the
peller shafts. The main turrets are 432 mm thick on
ir faces, 184 mm on their tops and 305 mm on their
cks and the barbettes upon which they are mounted
295 mm thick. There are three armoured decks, the
viest of which is 152 mm thick. After serving in

World War II the ships saw action in the Korean War and
New Jersey was briefly reactivated in 1968-9 off
Vietnam. In 1981 it was decided to recommission all
four as the centrepieces of four Surface Action Groups
(SAGs). Their combination of exceptionally high
protection by modern standards and long range heavy
artillery, coupled with the addition of modern missiles,
was considered to make them useful power projection
assets. Plans to give them further modifications were
shelved and reactivation was relatively cheap. BB61 and
BB63 were built in New York Navy Yard, being launched
on 27 August 1942 and 29 January 1944. BB62 and
BB64 were built in Philadelphia Navy Yard, being
launched on 7 December 1942 and 1944, respectively.

New Jersey was recommissioned on 28 December 1982.
Iowa recommissioned 8 April 1984, *Missouri* on 10 May
1986 and *Wisconsin* on 22 October 1988. Under the
Fiscal 1991 Budget, *New Jersey* and *Iowa*, which
suffered a serious turret explosion in 1989 are to be
decommissioned.

Photograph: *New Jersey* (HM Steele)

USA

Scale 1:2500

Specifications
and Technical Data

Displacement, tonnes: (Block 0) 9,743, (Block 1) 9,558, (Blocks 3-4) 9,618 full load
Dimensions, metres (feet): 172.5 × 16.8 × 9.5 (565.8 × 55 × 31)
Aircraft: (Block 0) 2 × SH-2F LAMPS I, (Blocks 1-4) 2 × SH-60 LAMPS III
Missiles: SAM: (Blocks 0-1) 2 × 2 Mk 26 launchers 68 Standard SM-2 MR or Standard SM-2 AEGIS ER (Blocks 2-4) Mk 41 Vertical Launch System fore and 61 missiles per launcher including Standard SM-2 MR Standard SM-2 MR and ER (Block IV)
SSM: 2 × 4 Harpoon aft, (Blocks 2-4) 20 Tomahawk SLCM, 8 carried in VLS
ASW: (Blocks 0-1) 20 ASROC for Mk 26 launchers, (Blocks 2-4) vertical launch ASROC when available
Guns: 2 × 1 127 mm, one forward one aft, 2 × 20 mm Vulcan Phalanx CIWS, one on each beam, 4 × 12.7 machine guns
Torpedoes: 2 × 3 324 mm Mk 32 tubes for 36 Mk 4 ASW LWT
Sonar: (Blocks 0-2) SQS 53 A/B medium-frequency, active search and attack, (CG54-5) SQR 19 low-frequency towed array, (Blocks 3-4) SQQ 89 combined hull-mounted and towed array
Radar: (Blocks 0-3) SPY 1A E/F band 3D air search and fire control phased array, (Block 4) SPY 1B, SPS 49(V)6 C/D band air search, SPS 55 I/J band surface search, (Block 0) LN 66, (Blocks 1-4) SPS 64 I band navigation, SPQ 9A and SPG 62 I/J band fire control
Action Information Organisation: CDS

umber in class: 27

ONDEROGA CG47 1983 A	MOBILE BAY CG53 1097 P	NORMANDY CG60 1989	SHILOH CG67 1991
KTOWN CG48 1984 A	ANTIETAM CG54 11987 P	MONTEREY CG61 1990	ANZIO CG68 1991
CENNES CG49 1985 P	LEYTE GULF CG55 1987 A	CHANCELLORSVILLE CG62 1989	VICKSBURG CG69 1992
LEY FORGE CG50 1986 A	SAN JACINTO CG56 1988 A	COWPENS CG63 1990	LAKE ERIE CG70 1992
OMAS C. GATES CG51	LAKE CHAMPLAIN CG57 1988 P	GETTYSBURG CG64 1990	CAPE ST GEORGE CG71 1993
987 P	PHILIPPINE SEA CG58 1989 A	CHOSIN CG65 1990	VELLA GULF CG72 1993
KER HILL CG52 1986 P	PRINCETON CG59 1989 P	HUE CITY CG66 1991	PORT ROYAL CG73 1993

chinery: 4 × General Electric LM 2500 gas turbines,
000 hp, 2 × shafts
eed, knots: 30 plus
nge, nautical miles: 6,000 at 20 knots
mplement: 358

se ships are the most capable anti-air warfare assets
at. The AEGIS weapon system is a combination of
ar and computers can handle 128 tracks
ultaneously at long range and can keep more than
lve missiles in the air at one time. It consists of 28
nputers controlling two separate radar systems, the
Y-1 for detection and tracking and the 4 Mk 80
minator-directors with their SPG 62 radars. These
omatically illuminate targets at the right time to home
he Standard missiles. The SM-2 MR has a range of
ut 40 nautical miles. The new Block IV ER missile,
cially built with a short booster for use with VLS will
more agile and have longer range. The class is
ded into 4 Blocks, Block 0 CG47-48, Block 1 CG49-
Block 2 CG52-55, Block 3 CG56-58, Block 4 CG59-
Each block has incremental improvement. Block 1
an improved helicopter, missiles, data displays and
suite. Block 2 introduced the Vertical Launch
tem, Block 3 the integrated ASW system and Block 4
hter version of SPY-1 new radar and computers. The
s, based on the 'Spruance' class destroyer hull
n, have been divided between the Ingalls
obuilding Corporation (CG47-50/52-57/59/62/65-6/
9/71-3) and Bath Ironworks. The first ship was laid
vn in January 1980 and the last one ordered in

February 1989. The ships cost in the region of $1 billion
each and have the modified version of NTDS called CDS
(Combat Data System or Command & Decision System)
integrated with the AEGIS Display System and the
Weapons Control System into the overall AEGIS weapon
system.

Photograph: *Mobile Bay* (HM Steele)
Silhouette: 'Ticonderoga' class blocks 0–1

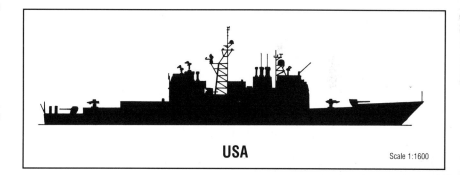

USA

Scale 1:1600

ecifications
d Technical Data

acement, tonnes: 11,481 full load
nsions, metres (feet): 117.3 × 19.2 × 9.6
7 × 63 × 31.5)
iles: SAM: 2 × 2 Mk 26 launchers, one forward, one
r 50 Standard SM-2 MR
2 × 4 Tomahawk SLCM aft, 2 × 4 Harpoon forward
, 16 ASROC in after missile magazine
: 2 × 127 mm, one forward, one aft, 2 × 20 mm
n Phalanx CIWS on each beam
edoes: 2 × 3 324 mm Mk 32 tubes for Mk 46
LWT
r: SQS 53A bow-mounted medium-frequency active
h and attack
r: SPS 48D/E E/F band 3D air search, SPS 40B or
49 C/D band air search, SPS 55 I/J band surface
h, LN 66 I/J band navigation, SPG 51D G/I band,
60D and SPQ 9A I/J band fire control
n Information Organisation: NTDS
inery: 2 × General Electric D2G pressurised water-
d reactors, 2 × geared turbines, 70, hp, 2 × shafts
d, knots: 30 plus
e, nautical miles: expected to operate 10 years
een fuellings
lement: (CGN38) 565, (CGN39) 572, (CGN40) 613,
41) 562

ally intended as nuclear-powered versions of the
3s they were completed as modified nuclear-powered
tes' (DLGN) with an emphasis on anti-air warfare.
ships were laid down at Newport News Shipbuilding
gust 1972, August 1973, February 1975 and January

1977 and were launched on 14 December 1974, 9 August 1975, 31 July 1976 and 21 October 1978. They were reclassified as cruisers at the end of June 1975 and CGN 41 was ordered as such. A fifth ship was projected, but was never built because of the advent of AEGIS. The original design had only one main missile launcher aft and this is reflected in the arrangement of SPG 51 main missile fire control radars at the aft end only and the larger after missile magazine, 44 round capacity instead of 24 forward. The 'Virginias' were originally fitted to carry a LAMPS helicopter in a stern hangar but this proved unsatisfactory in service and Tomahawk missile launchers were fitted instead in the 1980s. Kevlar armour was also added and the ships are undergoing New Threat Upgrade

modernisation which improves both the radar and integration of its outputs. This should be completed by the mid-1990s. The primary purpose of these vessels is the close escort of nuclear-powered aircraft carriers but their surface-to-surface missiles give them increased individual flexibility in the power projection role. The EW suite includes SRBOC flare and chaff launchers, the SLQ 32(V)3 combined ESM and jammer and the SLQ 25 Nixie torpedo decoy system.

Photograph: *Arkansas* (HM Steele)

USA

Scale 1:1100

CALIFORNIA CGN36 1974 P
SOUTH CAROLINA CGN37 1975 A

ecifications
d Technical Data

lacement, tonnes: 10,699 full load
ensions, metres (feet): 181.7 × 18.6 × 9.6
× 61 × 31.5)
raft: helicopter platform
siles: SAM: 2 × 1 Mk 13 launchers, one forward,
aft for 80 Standard SM-1 or SM-2 MR missiles
: 2 × 4 Harpoon, one amidships, one aft
: 1 × 8 ASROC forward, 24 missiles
s: 2 × 127 mm, one forward, one aft,
20 mm Vulcan Phalanx CIWS, one on each beam
edoes: 2 × 2 324 mm Mk 32 for Mk 46 ASW LWT
ar: SQS 26 bow-mounted medium-frequency active
ar: SPS 48C/E E/F band air search, SPS 40B or
49 C/D band air search, SPS 10 or SPS 67 G band
ace search, LN 66 I/J band navigation, SPG51D G/I
, SPG 60 and SPQ 9A I/J band fire control
on Information Organisation: NTDS
hinery: 2 × General Electric D2G pressurised water-
ed reactors, 2 × geared turbines, 70,000 hp,
shafts
ed, knots: 30
ge, nautical miles: limited only by endurance of

plement: (CGN36) 603, (CGN37) 595

e ships are nuclear-powered versions of an abortive
l 1966 guided missile destroyer design. Because of
cost the Department of Defense sought their
ellation but Congress insisted on their continuation.
rd ship became the first of the next class.
weight Mk 45 5-inch guns were mounted instead of

the intended Mk 42s. The SM-1 MR missiles combined the range of the earlier Terrier long-range system with a much higher rate of fire. They were originally classified as 'frigates' (DLGN), being reclassified cruisers in 1975. Their improved reactors had three times the core life of those of the previous DLGNs. They were both built by Newport News Shipbuilding, being laid down on 23 January 1970 and 1 December 1970 and launched on 22 September 1971 and 1 July 1972. Their operational effectiveness has recently been limited by their relatively old systems, but they are currently undergoing New Threat Upgrade refits which will greatly enhance their capacity in their primary role of providing close escort to nuclear-powered aircraft carriers. They

possess extraordinary powers of both strategic and tactical mobility as they can maintain high speeds for almost indefinite periods. The long thin hull form gives excellent seakeeping at high speed. Armour has been added to protect their upper works which has enhanced their tendency to roll and this can make using the helicopter pad for vertical replenishments difficult. It has been decided not to fit these ships with Tomahawk because of the topweight problem.

Photograph: *South Carolina* (HM Steele)

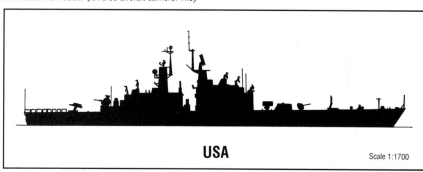

USA

Scale 1:1700

pecifications
d Technical Data

splacement, tonnes: 9,273 full load
ensions, metres (feet): 171.9 × 17.7 × 9.6
4 × 58 × 31)
craft: 1 × SH-2F LAMPS helicopter
siles: SAM: 1 × 2 Mk 10 launcher for 40 Standard
2 ER missiles aft
M: 2 × 4 Harpoon amidships
J: 20 ASROC ASW fired by SAM launcher
is: 1 × 127 mm forward, 2 × 20 mm Vulcan Phalanx
'S forward
pedoes: 2 × 2 Mk 32 tubes for Mk 46 ASW LWT
ar: SQS 26 bow-mounted medium-frequency active
ar: SPS 48E 3D E/F band air search, SPS 49 C/D
d air search, SPS 67 G band surface search,
66 I band navigation, SPG 53 I/J band and SPG 55B
band fire control
on Information Organisation: NTDS
hinery: 2 × General Electric D2G pressurised water-
ed reactors, 70,000 hp, 2 × shafts
ed, knots: 30
ge, nautical miles: limited only by endurance of
w
plement: 591

stinctive vessel with her two large lattice masts,
tun, the US Navy's second nuclear-powered 'frigate'
GN) was laid down at the Camden, New Jersey yard of
New York Shipbuilding Corporation on 17 June 1963.
was launched on 19 December 1964 and
missioned on 27 May 1967. She was essentially a
ear-powered version of the contemporary 'Belknap'

design which restored the flexibility of gun armament. The
major difference from the 'Belknaps' was that the main gun
was mounted forward and the missiles aft. Her main
improvement over the *Bainbridge* was the SQS 26 sonar
that necessitated the redesign. The ship carries a Mk 42
5-inch gun on the forecastle and originally also had a
secondary armament of two 76 mm guns. These were
replaced by Harpoon missiles in 1980. The ship also
carried two Mk 25 ASW heavyweight torpedo tubes at the
stern, but these did not prove successful and were later
removed. Vulcan Phalanx and a modern EW suite of
SRBOC chaff and flare launchers and the SLQ 32(V)3 and
SLQ 34 ESM and jamming system was fitted in 1982-4.
Truxtun underwent New Threat Upgrade modernisation in

Fiscal 1989. Her SM-2 ER missiles have a range of more
than 75 nautical miles. Despite these improvements, it has
been decided to decommission *Truxtun* as a cost-cutting
measure in 1994. She was reclassified CGN in 1975 along
with most of the other DL-type ships.

Photograph: *Truxtun* (HM Steele)

USA

Scale 1:1600

BELKNAP CG26 1964 A
JOSEPHUS DANIELS CG27 1965 A
WAINWRIGHT CG28 1966 A
JOUETT CG29 1966 P
HORNE CG30 1967 P
STERETT CG31 1967 P
WILLIAM H. STANDLEY CG32 1966 P

FOX CG33 1966 P
BIDDLE CG34 1967 A

ecifications
d Technical Data

lacement, tonnes: (CG26-28) 8,332,
9-33) 8,194, (CG34) 8,382
ensions, metres (feet): 166.7 × 16.7 × 8.8
× 54.8 × 28.8)
aft: (except CG26) SH-2F LAMPS I
iles: SAM: 1 × 2 Mk 10 launcher for Standard
2 ER
: 2 × 4 Harpoon
: 20 ASROC for Mk 10 launcher
: 1 × 127 mm aft, 2 × 20 mm Vulcan Phalanx
5 on each beam aft
edoes: 2 × 3 Mk 32 tubes for 18 Mk 46 ASW LWT
ar: SQS 26 or (CG26) SQS 53C bow-mounted
um-frequency active search and attack
ar: SPS 48C/E E/F band 3D air search, (CG26-30)
49(V)3 C/D band air search or (CG31-4) SPS 40 E/F
air search, SPS 67 G band surface search, LN 66 I
navigation, SPG 53F I/J band and SPG 55D G/H
fire control
n Information Organisation: NTDS
inery: 2 × General Electric or De Laval geared
nes, 4 × Babcock & Wilcox or Combustion
neering boilers, 85,000 hp, 2 × shafts
d, knots: 32.5
e, nautical miles: 8,000 at 14 knots,
0 at 30 knots
plement: 477 plus 11 flag staff in CG26

proved class of conventionally-powered DLGs built in
960s, they were originally intended to be more
ive versions of the DDG2 class destroyers with

improved sonar and greater range. As size increased they
became modified 'Leahy' DLs but their origins were
reflected in the return to a gun armament their being fitted
with the Drone Anti-Submarine Helicopter (DASH) system.
This has now been replaced by a LAMPS I helicopter
although an aircraft is not always carried. *Belknap* was
severely damaged in collision with the carrier *John F.
Kennedy* in November 1975 and was substantially rebuilt,
re-entering service in 1980 with improved radar, sonar and
missiles. Some of these modifications have been added to
other members of the class, but *Belknap* remains unique
as she was converted in 1985-6 with improved
accommodation and communications to serve as 6th Fleet
flagship. She is home ported at Gaeta, Italy for this duty.

The extra flag accommodation required the deletion of the
helicopter hangar. All the ships originally carried 3-inch
guns amidships but these were replaced by Harpoon
missiles from 1976 onwards. The SM-2 missiles have a
range of 75 nautical miles or more. Starting with CG34 the
ships are receiving New Threat Upgrade modernisation.
The builders were Bath Ironworks (CG26-28/32/34), Puget
Sound Naval Shipyard (CG29/31) San Francisco Naval
Shipyard (CG30) and Todd Shipyards, San Pedro (CG33).
They were all laid down between 5 February 1962 and
9 December 1963 and were launched between 20 July
1963 and 2 July 1965. They were rated cruisers in 1975.

Photograph: *Horne* (HM Steele)

USA

Scale 1:1500

Specifications and Technical Data

Displacement, tonnes: 8,730 full load
Dimensions, metres (feet): 172.3 × 17.6 × 9.5
(565 × 57.9 × 31.2)
Aircraft: helicopter pad aft
Missiles: SAM: 2 × 2 Mk 10, one forward, one aft for standard SM-2ER
SSM: 2 × 4 Harpoon aft
A/S: 1 × 8 ASROC forward
Guns: 2 × 20 mm Vulcan Phalanx CIWS on each beam midships
Torpedoes: 2 × 3 324 mm Mk 32 for ASW LWT
Sonar: SQQ 23 bow-mounted medium-frequency active search and attack
Radar: SPS 48E E/F band 3D air search, SPS 49 C/D band air search, SPS 67 G band surface search, LN 66 I band navigation, SPG 55C G/H band fire control
Action Information Organisation: NTDS
Machinery: 2 × General Electric D2G pressurised water-cooled reactors, 2 × geared turbines, 70,000 hp, 2 × shafts
Speed, knots: 30
Range, nautical miles: limited only by endurance of crew
Complement: 576

Design work on a nuclear-powered DLG similar to the conventionally-powered 'Leahy' class began at the beginning of 1957 in order to create all nuclear-powered task forces and overcome the escort range problem that was significant even with conventionally-powered carriers. A two reactor plant was required which

necessitated light cruiser dimensions. The *Bainbridge* was laid down by the Bethlehem Steel Company of Quincy, Mass. on 15 May 1959. She was launched on 15 April 1961 and commissioned on 6 October 1962. She was the US Navy's third nuclear-powered guided missile warship. She received a major modernisation at Puget Sound between 1974 and 1976 in which she was fitted with NTDS and improved guidance systems for her missiles. She also had her 3-inch guns removed, these later being replaced by Harpoon missiles. Another major modernisation took place in 1983-85 when the ship acquired her current appearance with a lattice mainmast. During this refit Phalanx CIWS was added, the missiles were upgraded to SM-2 standard and the current

electronic warfare suite fitted of SRBOC flare and chaff launchers and SLQ 32(V) and WLR 1 ESM/ECM. She is due to receive New Threat Upgrade modernisation in Fiscal 1990 but the decision has now been taken to decommission her in 1992 as part of the Fiscal 1991 defence cuts. She was reclassified CGN in 1975.

Photograph: *Bainbridge* (HM Steele)

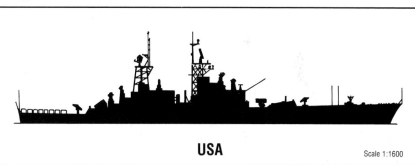

USA

Scale 1:1600

Number in class: 9

LEAHY CG16 1962 P
HARRY E. YARNELL CG17 1963 A
WORDEN CG18 1963 P
DALE CG19 1963 A
RICHMOND K. TURNER CG20 1964 A
GRIDLEY CG21 1963 P

ENGLAND CG22 1963 P
HALSEY CG23 1963 P
REEVES CG24 1964 P

Guided Missile Cruisers (CG)
Leahy Class

pecifications
nd Technical Data

placement, tonnes: 8,335 full load
nensions, metres (feet): 162.5 × 16.6 × 7.6
3 × 54.9 × 24.8)
craft: helicopter landing pad aft
ssiles: SAM: 2 × 2 Mk 10 launchers fore and aft for
Standard SM-2 ER
M: 2 × 4 Harpoon aft
W: 1 × 8 ASROC forward
ns: 2 × 20 mm Vulcan Phalanx CIWS aft
rpedoes: 2 × 3 324 mm Mk 32 for Mk 46 ASW LWT
nar: (CG17) SQQ 23 PAIR (remainder) SQS 23
w-mounted medium-frequency active search and
ack
dar: SPS 48 A/E E/F band 3D air search, SPS 49(V)3
band air search, SPS 10 or SPS 67 G band surface
rch, LN 66 I band navigation, SPG 55C G/H band fire
trol
ion Information Organisation: NTDS
chinery: 2 × General Electric or De Laval or
s-Chalmers geared turbines, 4 × Babcock & Wilcox
Foster Wheeler boilers, 85,000 hp, 2 × shafts
eed, knots: 32-33
nge, nautical miles: 8,000 at 20 knots
mplement: 423

signed in the late-1950s as highly advanced
missile fleet escort DLGs, they were laid down
ween 1959 and 1961 at Bath Iron Works, Maine
16-18), New York Shipbuilding, Camden (CG19-20),
jet Sound Bridge and Dry Dock Co. (CG21), Todd
pyards, San Pedro (CG22), San Francisco Naval

Shipyard (CG23) and Puget Sound Naval Shipyard
(CG24). Launch dates were: CG16 1 July 1961, CG17
31 May 1960, CG18 2 June 1862, CG19 28 July 1962,
CG20 6 April 1963, CG21 31 July 1961, CG22 6 March
1962, CG23 15 January 1962 and CG24 12 May 1962.
Their main armament was originally the Terrier missile
but this had been replaced by the Standard SM-1 ER by
1972 and the Standard SM-2 ER by 1985. These
missiles are all semi-active homers, but the autopilot in
the SM-2 allows an increase in range to 75 nautical
miles. Their only gun armament was two twin 3-inch on
each beam and these have been replaced by the Harpoon
launchers. The effectiveness of these ships was greatly
enhanced when NTDS automated action information

organisation was fitted at the same time as the Standard
missiles under the Fiscal 1966, 1967 and 1971
programmes. The radar on the 'Leahys' has also been
progressively upgraded and beginning with CG22 they
are receiving further, New Threat Upgrade
modernisation. This will allow them to serve as useful
task force AAW escorts until replacement by AEGIS
equipped vessels.

Photograph: *Harry E. Yarnell* (HM Steele)

USA

Scale 1:1500

pecifications
nd Technical Data

placement, tonnes: 17,806 full load
nensions, metres (feet): 219.9 × 22.3 × 9.1
1.2 × 73.2 × 29.7)
craft: helicopter landing pad aft
ssiles: SAM: 2 × 2 Mk 10 launchers forward for
Standard SM-2 ER forward
M: 2 × 4 Tomahawk SLCM aft, 2 × 4 Harpoon aft
W: 1 × 8 ASROC amidships
ns: 2 × 127 mm on each beam amidships,
20 mm Vulcan Phalanx CIWS aft
pedoes: 2 × 3 324 mm tubes for Mk 46 ASW LWT
iar: SQQ 23 PAIR medium-frequency hull-mounted
ve
dar: SPS 48C E/F band air search, SPS 49 C/D band
search, SPS 67 G band surface search, LN 66 I band
igation, SPG 55D G/H band and Mk 35 I/J band fire
trol
on Information Organisation: NTDS
chinery: 2 × Westinghouse pressurised
er-cooled reactors, 2 × General Electric geared
oines, 80,000 hp, 2 × shafts
ed, knots: 30
nge, nautical miles: limited only by endurance of
w
nplement: 1,026

only CGN designed as a proper cruiser rather than as
G (although even she was originally projected as a
lear-powered DL) *Long Beach* was laid down at the
hlehem Steel Yard at Quincy, Mass. on 2 December
7. She was launched on 14 July 1959 and

commissioned on 9 December 1961. She was originally
armed with Terrier missiles forward and the long-range
Talos missiles aft, with which she shot down two
aircraft at long range over Vietnam. Talos was,
however, deactivated in 1978 and removed the following
year. The ship received a major refit at Bremerton
between 1980 and 1983, when her forward Standard ER
missile system was uprated and the phased array SPS
32/33 radar which gave the ship her distinctive silhouette
was removed, although the prominent box-shaped
bridge structure remained. The 1980–83 refit replaced
a planned modernisation with AEGIS. The ship was
originally designed to be armed entirely with missiles,
including Regulus cruise missiles and even Polaris

SLBMs. These were never fitted in their planned
amidships position and the space was used instead for
two old Mk 30 5-inch gun mountings and their
associated directors. Tomahawk cruise missiles were
added on the stern in 1985 in armoured box launchers
causing the Harpoons, which had been fitted in 1980-83,
to be relocated on the after superstructure. The two
Vulcan Phalanx CIWS are mounted in place of the former
Talos radars. *Long Beach* has flagship facilities and is
due to receive New Threat Update modernisation to
enable her to continue to operate for some time.

Photograph: *Long Beach* (HM Steele)

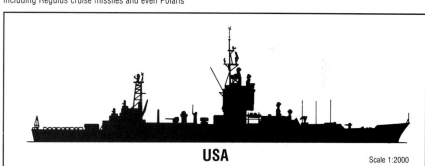

USA

Scale 1:2000

DES MOINES CA134 1948 A
SALEM CA139 1948 A

pecifications
nd Technical Data

splacement, tonnes: 21,815 full load
mensions, metres (feet): 218.5 × 23.3 × 7.9
16.5 × 76 × 26)
craft: helicopter facilities aft
ns: 3 × 3 203 mm, two forward, one aft,
× 2 127 mm, two forward, two on each beam,
9 × 2 76 mm on each beam and at stern (one
ounting forward in CA139)
dar: SG6 air search. SPS 8 height finding, (CA139)
S 12 air search, Mk 25, Mk 13, Mk 35 and (CA139)
34 and (CA134) SPG 50 fire control
chinery: 4 × General Electric geared turbines,
× Babcock & Wilcox boilers, 120,000 hp, 4 × shafts
eed, knots: 32
nge, nautical miles: 10,500 at 15 knots
mplement: 1,800

reserve at Philadelphia are these two old heavy
isers, the final examples of this traditional concept
lt. Both were laid down by Bethlehem Steel at Quincy,
ss. in mid-1945 and they were launched on
September 1946 and 25 March 1947. They displaced
much as the early 'Dreadnought' battleships and
ved to be impressive and successful flagships in their
ly years before being decommissioned on 30 January
59 (CA139) and 14 July 1961 (CA134). Their short
riod in first line service means that they are in
ellent structural condition and they have been kept in
rage for possible mobilisation as shore bombardment
sels. Their sister, USS *Newport News* (CA148), saw

extensive service in this role in the Vietnam War. She
was decommissioned in 1975 and stricken in 1978 but
remains moored alongside the other two vessels at
Philadelphia Navy Yard. The 203 mm (8-inch) guns are
rapid firing Mk 16s and can fire at 10 rounds per minute
per gun over a range of over 30,000 metres. The system
works successfully, although *Newport News* suffered an
accident off Vietnam. The ships are quite heavily
armoured with 152 mm belts, 25 mm and 85 mm deck
armour, 203 mm turret faces, 95 mm turret sides,
103 mm turret roofs and 160 mm barbettes. Given the
reactivation of the battleships after many years in
reserve, two of them close by these ships, it still seems
premature to write off these last heavy cruisers yet.

Photograph: *Salem* 1983 (PM Callaghan/USNI)

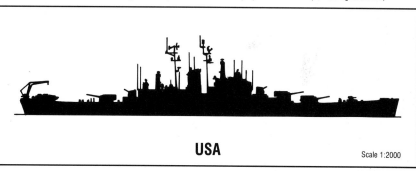

USA

Scale 1:2000

ARLEIGH BURKE DDG51 1991
BARRY DDG52 1991
JOHN PAUL JONES DDG53 1992
CURTIS WILBUR DDG54
STOUT DDG55
JOHN S. McCAIN DDG56
MITSCHER DDG57
LABOON DDG58

pecifications
d Technical Data

placement, tonnes: 8,535 full load
ensions, metres (feet): 153.6 c 20.4 × 9.1
4 × 66.9 × 29.6)
craft: fuelling and rearming platform for SH-60 Sea
k LAMPS III
siles: 2 × Mk 41 Vertical Launch Systems,
forward, 61 aft for Standard SM-2 MR or SM-2 ER
ckIV SAM, Tomahawk SLCM and vertical launch
ROC, 2 × 8 Harpoon SSM aft
s: 1 × 127 mm forward
pedoes: 2 × 3 324 mm tubes for Mk 46 ASW LWT
ar: SQQ 89 combined bow-mounted
ium-frequency active search and attack and
-frequency passive towed array
ar: SPY 1D E/F band 3D air search/fire control
sed array, SBS 67(V) G band surface search,
64 I band navigation, SPG 62 I/J band fire control
on Information Organisation: CDS
hinery: 4 × General Electric LM 2500-30 gas
ines, 100,000 hp, 2 × shafts
ed, knots: 30 plus
ge, nautical miles: 5,000 at 20 knots
plement: 303

'Arleigh Burke' class destroyers are intended to form
basis of the US Navy's surface ship procurement
the mid-1990s onwards. They will replace the
ing DDGs and CGs as battle group escorts. Like the
er CG47 class cruisers they are equipped with the
S anti-air warfare system which will allow them to
ge multiple targets. Considerable survivability

features have been incorporated in the design. Except for
the funnels they are to be built of steel and for the first
time in American warships they will have full nuclear,
biological and chemical (NBC) protection, a long-
standing feature in other navies. DDG51 was authorised
under the 1985 Fiscal Year programme and was laid
down on 6 December 1988 at Bath Ironworks, Maine.
She was launched on 16 September 1989 and is due to
commission at the end of March 1991. Two ships were
ordered in the Fiscal 1988 Budget and building DDG52
began at Ingalls Shipbuilding in March 1989. DDG53
was ordered from Bath Ironworks to be started in 1990.
She is due to commission in July 1992. The next four
ships of the class were all ordered on 13 December

1988, DDG54, 56 and 58 from Bath Ironworks and
DDG55 from Ingalls. Five ships a year are planned
thereafter, Congress permitting, but the programme has
run into difficulties because of increasing costs. DDG 51
is now costed at $1.2 billion and subsequent ships at
over $700 million each. The SSQ 89 sonar suite
combines an SQS 53C hull-mounted search and attack
set with an SQR 19 passive towed array.

Illustration: Artist's impression of *Arleigh Burke* (USNI)

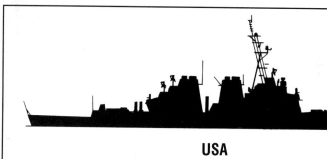

USA

Scale 1:1400

Number in class: 4

KIDD DDG993 1981 A
CALLAGHAN DDG994 1981 P
SCOTT DDG995 1981 A
CHANDLER DDG996 1982 P

Guided Missile Destroyers (DDG)
Kidd Class

ecifications
d Technical Data

placement, tonnes: 9,728 full load
ensions, metres (feet): 171.6 × 16.8 × 9.1
3 × 55 × 30)
raft: 2 × SH-2F LAMPS I
siles: SAM: 2 × 2 Mk 26 launchers for 52 Standard
1 MR, (DDG995) Standard SM-2 MR
M: 2 × 4 Harpoon amidships
W: 16 ASROC for Mk 26 launchers
s: 2 × 127 mm, one forward, one aft, 2 × 20 mm
an Phalanx CIWS
edoes: 2 × 3 324 mm Mk 32 tubes for
46 ASW LWT
ar: SQS 53A bow-mounted medium-frequency
ch and attack
ar: SPS 48C/E E/F band 3D air search, (DDG995
SPS 49 C/D band air search, SPS 55 I/J band
ace search, SPS 53 I/J band navigation, SPG 51D,
60 and SPQ 9A G/I/J band fire control
on Information Organisation: NTDS
hinery: 4 × General Electric LM 2500 gas turbines,
00 hp, 2 × shafts
ed, knots: 33
ge, nautical miles: 3,300 at 30 knots,
0 at 17 knots
plement: 339

e ships were designed for Iran in the 1970s, being
ed at the Ingalls Shipbuilding Corporation on
une 1978 (DDG993), 23 October 1978 (DDG994),
ebruary (DDG995) and 7 May 1979 (DDG996). The
nal names were *Kouroosh, Daryush, Nader* and

Anoushirvan. Originally two more ships were projected.
The Iranian contracts were cancelled in February and
March 1979 and the four ships were officially acquired
by the USN on 25 July 1979. The cost was $510 million
each, not a great deal for vessels of this capability. They
are basically the original American 'Spruance' design.
This was intended to be an air defence ship with a
companion ASW destroyer of lesser capability built on
the common hull. In the event the USN could not afford
guided missile destroyers in the numbers required for its
1970s destroyer replacement programme and built the
entire DD963 class as the cheaper ASW ships. The four
Iranian vessels were fortunate windfalls. DDG995 has
received New Threat Upgrade modernisation which

involved adding the SPS 49 radar and modifying the
missile control system for the longer range Standard
SM-2. The ship itself can conrol up to 20 of these
missiles or she can act aas a source of missiles for
accompanying AEGIS vessels. It is hoped to carry out
similar conversion to the rest of the class. Kevlar and
aluminium armour has been added to all ships to
enhance protection. The class has excellent air-
conditioning and is very suitable for tropical service.

Photograph: *Scott* 1984 (van Ginderern/USNI)

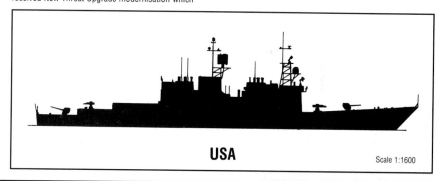

USA

Scale 1:1600

FARRAGUT DDG37 1960 A
LUCE DDG38 1961 A
MACDONOUGH DDG39 1961 A
COONTZ DDG40 1960 A
KING DDG41 1960 A
MAHAN DDG42 1960 A
DAHLGREN DDG43 1961 A

WILLIAM V. PRATT DDG44 1961 A
DEWEY DDG45 1960 A
PREBLE DDG46 1960 A

Guided Missile Destroyers (DDG)
Coontz Class

ecifications
d Technical Data

lacement, tonnes: 6,249 full load
ensions, metres (feet): 156.3 × 16 × 7.1
.5 × 52.5 × 23.4)
raft: helicopter landing pad aft
iles: SAM: 1 × 2 Mk 10 launcher for 40 Standard
2 ER aft
: 2 × 4 Harpoon aft
: 1 × 8 ASROC forward, (DDG37 carries 4 reloads)
s: 1 × 127 mm forward
edoes: 2 × 3 324 mm Mk 32 for Mk 46 ASW LWT
r: SQQ 23A PAIR hull-mounted medium-frequency
ch and attack
r: SPS 48C or (DDG42) SPS 48E E/F band 3D air
h, SPS 49(V) C/D band air search, SPS 10 G band
ce search, (DDG37/39/40/42/44) LN 66 I band
ation, or Pathfinder I band navigation, SPG 53 I/J
and SPG 55B G/H band fire control
n Information Organisation: NTDS
inery: 2 × De Laval or Allis-Chalmers geared
nes, 4 × Foster Wheeler or Babcock & Wilcox
rs, 85,000 hp, 2 × shafts
d, knots: 33
e, nautical miles: 5,000 at 20 knots
lement: 421

e were originally classified as frigates when they
built as specialised AAW/ASW task force escorts in
te 1950s. Their original numbering was DLG6-15.
the other DLGs and DLGNs were reclassified as
ers these became destroyers. They were given their
major modernisation between 1970 and 1977 which

saw their Terrier missiles replaced by Standard
SM-1 ER, NTDS fitted in all ships, improved radar and
the replacement of their four 3-inch guns by Harpoon
SSM launchers. DDG37 also received an ASROC reload
magazine, but this deleted in the other ships to save
weight. DDG42 was the trials ship for the New Threat
Upgrade modernisation which involved improved SPS
48 and 49 radar, the SYS-2 Integrated Automatic Target
Detection and Tracking (IADT) system and SM-2 ER
missiles. The other ships have not received this
complete fit but have been equipped with the new
missiles from 1987 onwards. These modifications have
allowed the ships to remain useful but the class began to
be withdrawn from service in October 1989. DDG37 and

40 were the first to be decommissioned and they will be
followed in 1990 by DDG45, in 1991 by DDG38, 41 and
44 and in 1992 by DDG43 and 46. All will have gone by
1993. The ships were built by Bethelehem Steel, Quincy
(DDG37-39), Puget Sound Naval Shipyard (DDG40-41),
San Francisco Naval Shipyard (DDG42), Philapdelphia
Naval Shipyard (DDG43-44) and Bath Ironworks, Maine
(DDG45-46). They were laid down between March 1957
and March 1958 and launched between July 1958 and
March 1960.

Photograph: *Luce* 1988 (USNI)

USA

Scale 1:1400

LES F. ADAMS DDG2
60 A
, KING DDG3 1961 A
RENCE DDG4 1962 A
DE V. RICKETTS DDG5
62 A
EY DDG6 1962 A

HENRY B WILSON DDG7 1960 P
LYNDEMcCORMICKDDG81961P
TOWERS DDG9 1961 P
SAMPSON DDG10 1961 A
SELLERS DDG11 1961 A
ROBISON DDG12 1961 P
HOEL DDG13 1962 P

BUCHANAN DDG14 1962 P
BERKELEY DDG15 1962 P
JOSEPH STRAUSS DDG16
1963 P
CONYNGHAM DDG17 1963 A
SEMMES DDG18 1962 A
TATTNALL DDG19 1963 A

GOLDSBOROUGH DDG20 1963 P
COCHRANE DDG21 1964 P
BENJAMIN STODDERT DDG22
1964 P
RICHARD E. BYRD DDG23
1964 A
WADDELL DDG24 1964 P

acement, tonnes: 4,092 full load
ensions, metres (feet): 133.2 × 14.3 × 6.1
× 47 × 20)
iles: SAM: (DDG2-14) 1 × 2 Mk 11 with 42 Standard
MR or (DDG15-24) 1 × 1 Mk 13 with 40 Standard
MR
: (DBG2-14) 4 or (DDG15-24) 6 Harpoon for SAM
cher
: 1 × 8 ASROC amidships (4 reloads in some)
: 2 × 127 mm fore and aft
edoes: 2 × 3 324 mm for Mk 46 ASW LWT
r: SQQ 23 or SQS 23 D hull-mounted (bow-mounted
DG20-24) medium-frequency active search and attack
r: SPS 52 B/C E/F band 3D air search, SPS 40B/D E/F
air search, SPS 10 G band surface search, LN 66 I
navigation, SPG 51C G/I band and SPG 53A or
19-20/22) SPG 60 and SPQ 9A fire control
n Information Organisation: (DD19-20/22) NTDS
iinery: 2 × General Electric or Westinghouse geared
nes, 4 × Babcock and Wilcox or Foster Wheeler
rs, 70,000, 2 × shafts
d, knots: 30 plus
e, nautical miles: 6,000 at 15 knots
plement: 360

e ships were designed in the 1950s, based on the
ng 'Forest Sherman' design but with a Tartar missile
her in place of the aft 127 mm (5-inch) gun. Later
els were fitted with an improved single arm launcher.
ships were laid down between 1 April 1958 and
ine 1962. Launch dates were from 23 April 1959 to

26 February 1963. Builders were Bath Iron Works, Maine (DDG2-3/10-11), New York Shipbuilding (DDG4-6/15-17), Defoe Shipbuilding (DDG7-8/12-13) Todd Shipyards, Seattle (DDG9/14/23-24), Avondale Marine Ways (DDG18-19) and Puget Sound Bridge and Dry Dock Co. (DDG20-22). Other ships of this type have been built for West Germany and Australia. The ships were later modified to fire Standard missiles and it was originally planned to modernise the whole class at the beginning of the 1980s. Only three ships were, however, converted, DDG19/20 and 22 which were modernised between 1981 and 1985. This involved new radars and fire control systems, SRBOC chaff launchers and, most importantly, NTDS automated action information organisation. These ships can direct three

missiles simultaneously and interact with other units. The other ships have had their radar and electronic counter-measures updated as they have been overhauled and digital fire control systems were fitted in DDG4-6/8-12/15/18/21. Lack of NTDS remains a major drawback however and withdrawal of the 'Charles F Adams' class began in late 1989 with DDG2, 7, 11 and 13. It is continuing in 1990 with DDG3, 4, 5, 6, 8, 12, 16 and 23. DDG10, 14, 15, 17, 18, 19, 22 and 24 will decommission in 1991-92. The last will go in 1993.

Photograph: *Berkeley* (USNI)

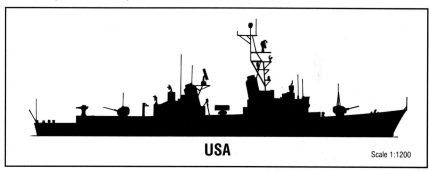

USA

Scale 1:1200

RUANCE DD963 1975 A
L F. FOSTER DD964 1976 P
KAID DD965 1976 P
VITT DD966 1976 P
IOTT DD967 1976 P
THUR W. RADFORD DD968
977 A
ERSON DD969 1977 A
RON DD970 1977 A

DAVID R. RAY DD971 1977 P
OLDENDORF DD972 1978 P
JOHN YOUNG DD973 1978 P
COMTE DE GRASSE DD974
    1978 A
O'BRIEN DD975 1977 P
MERRILL DD976 1978 P
BRISCOE DD977 1978 A
STUMP DD978 1978 A

CONOLLY DD979 1978 A
MOOSBRUGGER DD980 1978 A
JOHN HANCOCK DD981 1979 A
NICHOLSON DD982 1979 A
JOHN RODGERS DD983 1979 A
LEFTWICH DD984 1979 P
CUSHING DD985 1979 P
HARRY W. HILL DD986 1979 P
O'BANNON DD987 1979 A

THORN DD988 1980 A
DEYO DD989 1980A
INGERSOLL DD990 1980 P
FIFE DD991 1980 P
FLETCHER DD992 1980 P
HAYLER DD997 1983 A

placement, tonnes: 8,169 full load
nensions, metres (feet): 171.7 × 16.8 × 8.8
3.2 × 55.1 × 29)
craft: 2 × SH-2F LAMPS I or 1 × SH-60B LAMPS III
4 × SH-3 Sea King
ssiles: SAM: 1 × 8 Sea Sparrow aft,
0971) 1 × 10 RAM at stern
M: 2 × 4 Harpoon amidships, (DD974/6/9/83-4/90)
× 4 Tomahawk SLCM forward, (DD963/6-8 and later
os on refit) Mk 41 Vertical Launch System with up to
Tomahawk
W: 1 × 8 ASROC forward, 24 missiles to be replaced
vertical launch ASROC in VLS ships
ns: 1 × 2 127 mm, one forward, one aft,
× 20 mm Vulcan Phalanx CIWS, 4 × 12.7 mm
chine guns
pedoes: 2 × 3 324 mm Mk 32 for Mk 46 ASW LWT
ar: SQS 53 bow-mounted medium-frequency active
rch and attack, SQR 15 or SQR 19 low-frequency
sive towed array
dar: SPS 40 or DD 997, SPS 49 E/F band air search,
S 55 I/J band surface search, LN 66 I band
igation, SPG 60, SPQ 9A and Mk 31 I/J band fire
itrol, Mk 23 I/J band Target Acquisition System
ion Information Organisation: NTDS
chinery: 4 × General Electric LM 2500 gas turbines,
000 hp, 2 × shafts
eed, knots: 33
nge, nautical miles: 3,300 at 30 knots,
00 at 17 knots
nplement: 334

This large class was built to replace the numerous World War II destroyers facing block obsolescence in the 1970s. They are task force escorts optimised for anti-submarine warfare although when equipped with 61 cell forward VLS launcher, first fitted in DD963 in 1986-87, they are acquiring a substantial anti-surface capability also. The VLS sytems will also carry ASROC ASW missiles when these are developed for vertical launch and perhaps also surface-to-air missiles for control by AEGIS-equipped ships in the force. This will restore AAW capability originally intended for the design. DD997 was an extra ship originally intended as an air-capable vessel carrying helicopters and STOV/L aircraft. This plan was abandoned and the ship completed as a standard 'Spruance' with

slightly revised radar. The rest of the class was built under a single contract by the Ingalls Shipbuilding Division of Litton Industries of Pascagoula, Mississippi. DD997's contract was placed with Ingalls in 1979. Work on DD963 began in 1972 and she was launched on 10 November 1973; DD992, was launched on 16 June 1979. DD997 was begun on 20 October 1980 and launched on 27 March 1982. The ships were built on the modular basis in order to make construction easier and to allow convenient modernisation. Considerable room was left in the ships for extra systems should these be required.
Photograph: *Oldendorf* (foreground) and *Paul F. Foster* (HM Steele)
Silhouette: *Spruance* with VLS

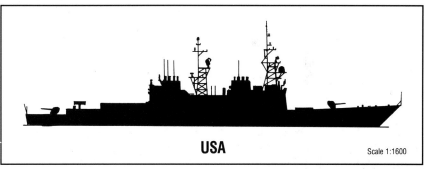

USA

Scale 1:1600

FORREST SHERMAN DD931
  1955 A
DAVIS DD937 1957 A
MANLEY DD940 1957 A
DUPONT DD941 1947 A
BIGELOW DD942 1957 A
BLANDY DD943 1957 A

MULLINIX DD944 1958 A
MORTON DD948 1959 P
RICHARD S. EDWARDS DD950
  1959 P
TURNER JOY DD951 1959 P

ecifications
d Technical Data

placement, tonnes: 4,115-4,156 full load
ensions, metres (feet): 127.5 × 13.7 × 6.7
3 × 45 × 22)
V: 1 × 8 ASROC in DD937/40-1/43/48/50
s: 3 (or ASROC ships) 2 × 127 mm, one forward,
 aft
pedoes: 2 × 3 324 mm torpedo tubes for ASW LWT
ar: SQS 23 hull-mounted medium-frequency active
rch and attack, SQS 35 variable depth active in
ROC ships
ar: SPS 37 P band or SPS 40 F/G band air search,
5 10 G band surface search, Mk 35 and SPG 53 I/J
d fire control
hinery: 2 × General Electric or Westinghouse
ed turbines, 4 × Foster Wheeler or Babcock and
cox boilers, 70,000 hp, 2 × shafts
ed, knots: 32.5
ge, nautical miles: 4,500 at 20 knots
plement: 298-306

remaining ships of the first American class of
-war destroyer are retained in reserve for possible
 as shore bombardment vessels. Their three single
42 automatic 5-inch mounts gave greater firepower
 longer range than double the number of guns
ied in World War II destroyers. DD931, 943, 944
951 are in original condition, the others were given
 conversions with ASROC and variable depth sonar.
eral ships have been stricken, the *Barry* (DD933)
 exhibited at Washington Navy Yard, the *Jonas*
ram (DD938) used as an engineering test hulk at

Philadelphia, the *Hull* (DD945) used as a target and the
Edson (DD946) placed for disposal at the end of 1988
after being used as Naval Reserve and Officer Candidate
School training ship at Newport, Rhode Island. Four
ships converted to DDGs with a Tartar/ASROC launcher
aft, the *John Paul Jones* (DD932/DDG32), *Decatur*
(DD963/DDG31), *Somers* (DD947/DDG34) and *Parsons*
(DD949/DDG33) have also been stricken. The surviving
ships were built by Bath Iron Works (DD931/940-2),
Bethlehem Steel (DD937/44-6), Ingalls Shipbuilding
(DD948) and Puget Sound Shipbuilding and Dry Dock
Co. (DD950-1). Despite being kept it seems unlikely that
these old ships will see further service as they were not
overhauled before they were placed in mothballs.

Photograph: *Turner Joy* 1980 (van Ginderen/USNI)
Silhouette: 'Forrest Sherman' class unmodified version

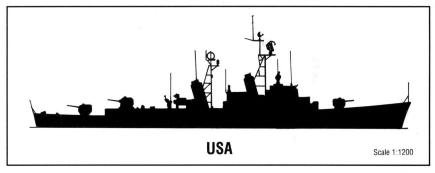

USA

Scale 1:1200

81

Number in class: 51

OLIVER HAZARD PERRY FFG7
1977 A
McINERNEY FFG8 1979 A
WADSWORTH FFG9 1980 P
DUNCAN FFG10 1980 P
CLARK FFG11 1980 A
GEORGE PHILIP FFG12
1980 P

SAMUEL ELIOT MORISON FFG13
1980 A
JOHN H. SIDES FFG14 1981 P
ESTOCIN FFG15 1981 A
CLIFTON SPRAGUE FFG16 1981 A
JOHN A. MOORE FFG19 1981 P
ANTRIM FFG20 1981 A
FLATLEY FFG21 1981 A

FAHRION FFG22 1982 A
LEWIS B. PULLER FFG23 1982 P
JACK WILLIAMS FFG24 1981 A
COPELAND FFG25 1982 P
GALLERY FFG26 1981 A
MAHLON S. TISDALE FFG27
1982 P
BOONE FFG28 1982 A

STEPHEN W. GROVES FFG29
1982 A
REID FFG30 1983 P
STARK FFG31 1982 A
JOHN L. HALL FFG32 1982 A
JARRETT FFG33 1983 P
AUBREY FITCH FFG34 1982 A
UNDERWOOD FFG36 1983 A

OMMELIN FFG37 1983 P
RTS FFG38 1983 P
YLE FFG39 1983 A
YBURTON FFG40 1984 A
LUSKY FFG41 1983 P
KRING FFG42 1983 A
CH FFG43 1984 P
WERT FFG45 1983 A

RENTZ FFG46 1984 P
NICHOLAS FFG47 1984 A
VANDEGRIFT FFG48 1984 P
ROBERT G. BRADLEY FFG49
  1985 A
TAYLOR FFG50 1984 A
GARY FFG51 1984 P
CARR FFG52 1985 A

HAWES FFG53 1985 A
FORD FFG54 1985 P
ELROD FFG55 1985 A
SIMPSON FFG56 1985 A
REUBEN JAMES FFG57 1986 P
SAMUEL B. ROBERTS FFG58
  1986 A
KAUFFMAN FFG59 1987 A

RODNEY M. DAVIS FFG60 1987 P
INGRAHAM FFG61 1989 P

placement, tonnes: (FFG7/FFG9-35) 3,643,
mainder) 4,166 full load
nensions, metres (feet): (FFG7/9-34) 135.6,
mainder) 138.1 × 13.7 × 7.5
5/453 × 45 × 24.5)
craft: (FFG7/9-35) 2 × SH-2F LAMPS I, (remainder)
: SH-60B LAMPS III helicopters
ssiles: 1 × Mk 13 launcher forward for 36 Standard
-1 MR SAM and 4 × Harpoon SSM
ns: 1 × 76 mm amidships, 1 × 20 mm Vulcan
alanx CIWS aft
pedoes: 6 × 324 mm Mk 32 tubes
Mk 46 ASW LWT
nar: SQS 56 hull-mounted medium-frequency search
attack, SQR 18A or SQR 19 low-frequency passive
ved array
dar: SPS 49(V) 2 or 5 C/D band air search,
5 55 I/J band surface search, STIR and Mk 92 I/J
d fire control
lon Information Organisation: UYK7/UYK4
chinery: 2 × General Electric LM 2500 gas turbines,
000 hp, 1 × shaft, 2 × 325 hp retractable pods for
ergency propulsion
eed, knots: 29
nge, nautical miles: 4,500 at 20 knots
mplement: 206

s large class was designed in the 1970s to primarily to
tect merchant shipping. FFG7 was originally a 'patrol
ate' but the designation was changed shortly after she
s laid down at Bath Iron Works, Maine in June 1975.

Bath shared construction with Todd Shipyards at San
Pedro and Seattle. Bath ships were FFG728/11/13/15-6/21/
24/26/29/32/34/36/39/42/45/47/49-50/53/55-6/58-9. San
Pedro ships are FFG9/12/14/19/23/25/27/30/33/38/41/43/
46/51/54,57/60-1 and Seattle ships are FFG10/20/22/28/
31/37/40/48/52. The missing numbers in the American
series are taken up by four ships built for Australia in
1980-83. Eighteen ships have been transferred to the Naval
Reserve Force between 1984 and 1990. These are FFG7/9-
16/19-27. The lengthened ships can operate the LAMPS III
helicopter using the Rapid Hauldown and Traversing
(RAST) system. It was originally planned to build 75 of
these ships but the Reagan Administration preferred to
emphasise fleet vessels for forward deployment and cut

the class at fifty ships. Congress voted an extra frigate,
FFG61, in the Fiscal 1984 Budget. Operational vessels
carry the SQR 19 towed arraay which greatly enhances the
ASW capacity of the class. Combat experience in the Gulf
has led to improvements in the survivability of these ships
and improved damage control techniques. These ships
were not given NTDS with its interactive capability with
other ships but carry the system's UYK-7 and UYK-4
computers to automate and integrate their own systems.
Data links are now being provided to non-NRF ships to give
full NTDS capability.

Photograph: *George Philip* (HM Steele)

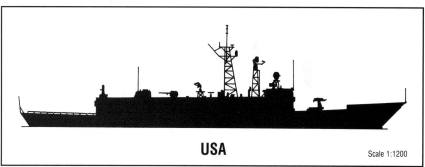

USA

Scale 1:1200

Number in class: 46

KNOX FF1052 1969 P
ROARK FF1053 1969 P
GRAY FF1054 1970 P
HEPBURN FF1055 1969 P
CONNOLE FF1056 1969 A
RATHBURNE FF1057 1970 P
MEYERKORD FF1058 1969 P

W.S. SIMS FF1059 1970 A
LANG FF1060 1970 P
PATTERSON FF1061 1970 A
WHIPPLE FF1062 1970 P
REASONER FF1063 1971 P
LOCKWOOD FF1064 1970 P
STEIN FF1065 1972 P

MARVIN SHIELDS FF1066 P
FRANCIS HAMMOND FF1067
   1970 P
VREELAND FF1068 1970 A
BAGLEY FF1069 1982 P
DOWNS FF1070 1971 P
BADGER FF1071 1970 P

BLAKELY FF1072 1970 A
ROBERT E. PEARY FF1073
   1972 P
HAROLD E. HOLT FF1074
   1971 P
TRIPPE FF1075 1970 A
FANNING FF1076 1971 P

ELLET FF1077 1970 P
SEPH HEWES FF1078 1971 A
WEN FF1079 1971 A
JL FF1080 1971 A
LWIN FF1081 1971 A
MER MONTGOMERY FF1082 1971 A

COOK FF1083 1971 P
McCANDLESS FF1084 1972 A
DONALD B. BEARY FF1085 1972 A
BREWTON FF1086 1972 P
KIRK FF1087 1972 P
BARBEY FF1088 1972 P

JESSE L. BROWN FF1089 1973 A
AINSWORTH FF1090 1973A
MILLER FF1091 1973 A
THOMAS C. HART FF1092 1973 A
CAPODANNO FF1093 1973 A

PHARRIS FF1094 1974 A
TRUETT FF1095 1974 A
VALDEZ FF1096 1974 A
MOINESTER FF1097 1974 A

splacement, tonnes: (FF1052-1077) 3,960, (remainder) 328 full load

mensions, metres (feet): 133.5 × 14.3 × 7.8 (38 × 46.8 × 24.8)

craft: 1 × SH-2F LAMPS I helicopter

ssiles: SSM: Harpoon missiles fired from 2 cells of ROC launcher

W: 1 × 8 ASROC launcher forward, 8 reloads, mix of rpoon and ASROC

ns: 1 × 127 mm forward, 1 × 20 mm Vulcan Phalanx WS on stern

rpedoes: 2 × 2 324 mm Mk 32 for Mk 46 ASW LWT

nar: SQS 26 bow-mounted medium-frequency active rch and attack, SQS 35 variable depth active, SQR 17 or low fequency passive towed array

dar: SPS 40 E/F band air search or (FF1070) Mk 23 D nd Target Acquisition System, SPS 10 or SPS 67 G band rface search, LN 66 I band navigation. SPF 53A I/J band control

chinery: 1 × Westinghouse geared turbine, × Combustion Engineering or Babcock and Wilcox lers, 35,000 hp, 1 × shaft

eed, knots: 27

nge, nautical miles: 4,500 at 20 knots

mplement: 288

ge oceangoing convoy escorts, these ships were ginally numbered in the DE series. The designation was anged from ocean escort to frigate in 1975. Construction s shared between Todd Shipyards at Seattle and San dro, and Avondale Shipyards at New Orleans with a few

ships build by Lockheed Shipbuilders at Seattle. Avondale ships were FF1056/59/61/68/72/75/77-97, Todd Seattle ships were FF1052-54/62/64/66/70-71, Todd San Pedro ships were FF1055/58/60/67/74/76 and Lockheed ships were FF1063/65/69/73. The ships were laid down between 5 October 1965 and 25 August 1972. They were launched between 19 November 1966 and 12 May 1973. One reason for the increase in size was the use of non-pressure-fired boilers. The prominent 'mack' was designed to carry an EW suite that was never in fact developed. Current EW fit is four SRBOC flare and chaff launchers and an SLQ 32(V)2 combined ESM/ECM. Ships equipped with VDS carry the SQR 18A(V)1 towed array. The (V)2 variant is carried in those without VDS. 31 of these ships carried a Sea

Sparrow missile launcher aft until it was replaced by Vulcan Phalanx. These ships were originally designed to carry Mk 25 heavyweight torpedo tubes in the stern. FF1053-5/ 58-60/72/90-1/96, have been transferred to the Naval Reserve Force and fourteen more are due to follow by 1993. Lack of automated AIO is a real drawback of these ships. A Service Life Extension Program (SLEP) including fitting the FF Shipboard Integrated Data System (FFISTS) is being considered. The bow bulwarks were extended in these ships to improve seakeeping.

Photograph: *Truett* 1988 (William Lipski/USNI)

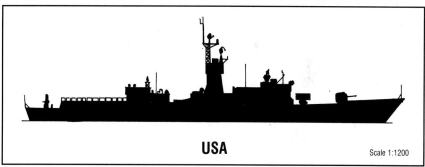

USA

Scale 1:1200

pecifications
nd Technical Data

placement, tonnes: 3,481 full load
mensions, metres (feet): 126.3 × 13.5 × 7.3
4.5 × 44.2 × 44)
ssiles: ASW: 1 × 8 ASROC forward
ns: 1 × 127 mm forward
pedoes: 2 × 3 Mk 32 tubes for Mk 46 ASW LWT
nar: SQS 26 AXR bow-mounted medium-frequency
ve search and attack
dar: SPS 40 E/F band air search, SPS 10 G band
face search, LN 66 I band navigation, Mk 35 I/J band
control
chinery: 1 × Westinghouse geared turbine,
× Foster Wheeler boilers, 35,000 hp, 1 × shaft
eed, knots: 27 knots
nge, nautical miles: 4,000 at 20 knots
mplement: 235

s vessel was authorised in the Fiscal 1961 Program
a research ship to test pumpjet propulsion. She was
down at Bath Ironworks, Maine on 29 July 1963,
nched on 17 April 1965 and commissioned on
November 1965. Her original designation was escort
earch ship (AGDE1) changed to frigate research ship
FF1) in June 1975. As the ship began to undertake
erational missions she was numbered as a frigate at
end of the 'Knox' class series in 1979. She is
erally similar to the now stricken 'Brooke' and
rcia' class FFGs and FFs but has extra
ommodation for research teams in the after part of
ship. The stern is raised to house the VDS. Two
25 stern torpedo tubes were originally fitted but have

been removed. The gun is of the older Mk 30 type.
Glover is still used for experiments which accounts for
her retention in service. The sixteen 'Garcias' and
'Brookes' were early victims of the squeeze on American
defence spending and they were decomissioned in Fiscal
1988 and 1989 and offered for sale. Eight were sold to
Pakistan and three to Brazil and the other five may also
find buyers among America's allies. They were fitted
with pressure fired boilers which proved troublesome in
service.

Photograph: *Glover* (HM Steele)

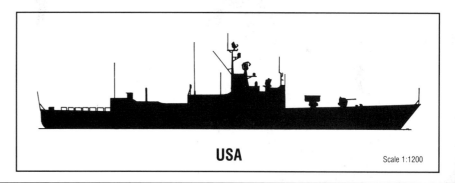

USA

Scale 1:1200

Number in class: 2

BRONSTEIN FF1037 1963 P
McCLOY FF1038 1963 A

ecifications
d Technical Data

lacement, tonnes: 2,693 full load
ensions, metres (feet): 113.2 × 12.3 × 7
.5 × 40.5 × 23)
raft: helicopter landing pad aft
siles: ASW: 1 × 8 ASROC forward
s: 1 × 2 76 mm forward
edoes: 2 × 3 324 mm Mk 32 tubes for
6 ASW LWT
ar: SQS 26 AXR medium-frequency bow-mounted
e search and attack
ar: SPS 40 E/F band air search, SPS 10 G band
ace search, LN 66 I band navigation, Mk 35 I/J band
control
hinery: 1 × De Laval geared turbine, 2 × Foster
eler boilers, 20,000 hp, 1 × shaft
ed, knots: 26 knots
ge, nautical miles: 4,000 at 15 knots
plement: 215

ugh the oldest of the 1960s generation of DEs, the
nstein' class are the last of the pre-'Knox' class
els to remain in service (apart from the research
te *Glover*). The ships were originally fitted with the
H Drone Helicopter System and a second pair of
m guns aft. The after guns were removed when the
ships were converted to carry the SQR 15 towed
. This has now been removed. Their more reliable
nore easily maintained low pressure steam
oment accounts in part for their remaining in the
e inventory for coastal patrol and surveillance
s. The troublesome pressure fired boilers of the

later 'Garcia' and 'Brooke' classes were a major reason
for their early decommissioning and sale. The two
'Bronsteins' were always considered too small and slow
for ocean-going ASW work and later DE classes were
larger and faster. Given the squeeze on the US defence
budget they may well not last much longer. Both were
built by Avondale Shipyards, being laid down
respectively on 16 May 1961 and 15 September 1961.
They were launched on 31 March 1962 and 9 June 1962
and commissioned on 16 June 1963 and 21 October
1963.

Photograph: *McCloy* 1987 (David Smith/USNI)

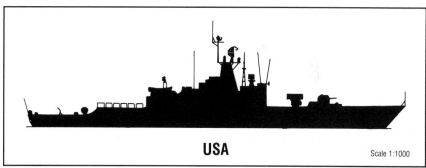

USA

Scale 1:1000

HAMILTON WHEC715 1967 A
DALLAS WHEC716 1967 A
MELLON WHEC717 1967 A
CHASE WHEC718 1968 A
BOUTWELL WHEC719 1968 A
SHERMAN WHEC720 1968 P
GALLATIN WHEC721 1968 P

MORGENTHAU WHEC722 1969 P
RUSH WHEC723 1969 P
MUNRO WHEC724 1971 P
JARVIX WHEC725 1971 P
MIDGETT WHEC726 1972 P

pecifications
d Technical Data

placement, tonnes: 3,099 full load
ensions, metres (feet): 115.2 × 13.1 × 6.1
8 × 42.8 × 20)
raft: 1 × HH 65A helicopter or LAMPS I
s: 1 × 127 mm being replaced in FRAM ships by
76 mm forward, 2 × 1 20 mm, 4 × 12.7 mm
chine guns and 2 × 40 mm grenade launchers
pedoes: 2 × 3 324 mm tubes for Mk 46 ASW LWT
ar: SQS 38 hull-mounted medium-frequency active
rch and attack, towed array in FRAM ships
lar: SPS 29 B/C band , in FRAM ships SPS 40 E/F
d air search, SPS 64(V) I band surface search,
35, in FRAM ships Mk 92 fire control
chinery: 2 × Fairbanks Morse 38 DT8 diesels,
00 hp, 2 × Pratt and Whitney FT4-A6 gas turbines,
000 hp, 2 × shafts
ed, knots: 29
ge, nautical miles: 14,000 at 11 knots on diesels,
00 at 29 knots on gas turbines
plement: 151

gest of the US Coastguard cutters, these are
ctively frigates and their military capabilities are
g enhanced as they undergo a Fleet Rehabiltation
Modernisation (FRAM) programme. This is being
ied out at the Todd Shipyard, Seattle for the West
st ships and Bath Ironworks, Maine for the East
st based vessels. *Hamilton* was the first to undergo
process, arriving at Bath in October 1985 and
mmissioning in June 1989. The rest of the class
uld be complete by December 1992. The FRAM

conversion will allow the operation of the LAMPS I
helicopter and the ships will be fitted for, but not with,
Harpoon surface-to-surface missiles and Vulcan Phalanx
CIWS. SRBOC chaff and flare launchers and an SLQ
32(V)2 ESM/ECM will be fitted along with Nixie torpedo
decoys. At the direction of the President these vessels
could pass under Naval command and would be very
useful additions to the United States' inventory of
escorts. The earlier ships of the class were originally
fitted with Hedgehog ahead throwing ASW weapons but
these have been removed. In normal circumstances the
high endurance cutters are used for such duties as anti-
drug patrols. They were all built by Avondale Shipyards
of New Orleans being laid down between 1965 and 1971.

Launch dates were WHEC715 18 December 1965,
WHEC716 1 October 1966, WHEC717 11 February 1967,
WHEC718 20 May 1967, WHEC719 17 June 1967,
WHEC720 23 September 1967, WHEC721 18 November
1967, WHEC722 10 February 1968, WHEC723
16 November 1968, WHEC724 5 December 1970,
WHEC725 24 April 1971 and WHEC726 4 September
1971.

Photograph: *Mellor* 1987 (Todd Shipyards/USNI)

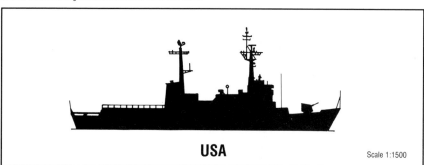

USA

Scale 1:1500

BEAR WMEC901 1983 A
TAMPA WMEC902 1983 A
HARRIET LANE WMEC903 1984 A
NORTHLAND WMEC904 1984 A
SPENCER WMEC905 1986 A
SENECA WMEC906 1986 A
ESCANABA WMEC907 1987 A

TAHOMA WMEC908 1987 A
CAMPBELL WMEC909 1988 A
THESTIS WMEC910 1988 A
FORWARD WMEC911 1989 A
LEGARE WMEC912 1989 P
MOHAWK WMEC913 1990 P

Medium Endurance Coast Guard Cutters (WMEC)
Famous Cutter Class

Specifications and Technical Data

Displacement, tonnes: 1,752 full load
Dimensions, metres (feet): 82.3 × 11.6 × 4.1
(270 × 38 × 13.5)
Aircraft: 1 × HH-65A or LAMPS helicopter
Guns: 1 × 76 mm forward, 2 × 12.7 mm machine
guns, 2 × 40 mm grenade launchers
Radar: SPS 64(V) I/K band surface search, Mk 92 fire
control
Machinery: 2 × Alco 251 diesels, 7,000 hp, 2 shafts
Speed, knots: 19.5
Range, nautical miles: 9,500 at 13 knots
Complement: 116

A modern class of cutter built to replace earlier high and
medium endurance cutters. Although these ships would
be employed as escorts in wartime, it was decided not to
give them the originally intended towed array sonar,
Harpoon missiles or CIWS although these might be fitted
in wartime. In war situtions the main combat capability
would come from the LAMPS helicopter, for which they
are fitted with a telescopic hangar, the only medium
endurance cutters so equipped. The gun is the rapid
firing OTO-Melara weapon fitted to the larger 'Hamilton'
class cutters after FRAM and the EW fit comprises
SBOC chaff launchers and SLQ 32(V)2 ESM/ECM.
Diesel engines were chosen to provide long patrol
endurance. Their low length-to-beam ratio does not
make for good sea keeping in Atlantic conditions. They
are intended for two week law enforcement patrols out to
ranges of 400 miles. Their maximum endurance is three
weeks. The ship were originally ordered from the

Tacoma Boatbuilding Company, the first being laid down
on 23 August 1979. Launch dates for the first four were
25 September 1980, 19 March 1981, 6 February 1982,
and 7 May 1982. Robert E Direktor Corporation of
Middletown Rhode Island threatened to sue if the other
contracts were not put to competitive bidding and the
rest of the class were built there. The first two Direktor
cutters were launched on 17 April 1984. The others were
launched in pairs on 6 February 1985, 29 April 1986 and
22 August 1987, with last of the class launched alone on
5 May 1988. These ships are sometimes known as the
'Bear' Class.

Photograph: *Seneca* 1987 (A Sheldon-Duplaix/Naval Forces)

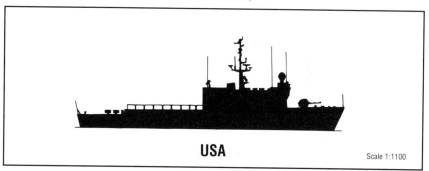

USA

Scale 1:1100

RELIANCE WMEC615 1964 A
DILIGENCE WMEC616 1964 A
VIGILANT WMEC617 1964 A
ACTIVE WMEC618 1966 P
CONFIDENCE WMEC619 1966 A
RESOLUTE WMEC620 1966 P
VALIANT WMEC621 1967 A
COURAGEOUS WMEC622 1968 A

STEADFAST WMEC623 1968 A
DAUNTLESS WMEC624 1968 A
VENTUROUS WMEC625 1968 P
DEPENDABLE WMEC626 1968 A
VIGOROUS WMEC627 1969 A
DURABLE WMEC628 1967 A
DECISIVE WMEC629 1968 A
ALERT WMEC630 1969 A

Medium Endurance Coast Guard Cutters (WMEC)
Reliance Class

pecifications
nd Technical Data

splacement, tonnes: (A Class) 1,128, (B Class) 1,147 load
mensions, metres (feet): 64.2 × 10.4 × 3.2
0.5 × 34 × 10.5)
craft: Pad for HH-65A helicopter
ns: 1 × 76 mm forward, 2 × 12.7 mm machine
ns, 2 × 40 mm grenade launchers
dar: SPS 64 (V) I band surface search
chinery: Alco 251E diesels, 5000 hp, two shafts
eed, knots: 18
nge, nautical miles: 6,100 at 14 knots
mplement: 71

It in two groups the A Class (615-619) and the B
ss. The As were launched between May 1963 and
y 1965, the first three by Todd of Seattle and the
er two by the Christy Corporation of Sturgeon Bay,
sconsin, and the Coast Guard Yard at Curtis Bay,
ryland. They had a combined gas turbine and diesel
wer unit. The Solar Saturn gas turbines were later
moved leaving the 3,000 hp Cooper-Bessemer diesels.
ese are being replaced by Alco 251s when the ships
dergo MMA (Major Maintenance Availability) refits at
Coast Guard Yard — WMEC618 began the first MMA
1984 and completed it in 1987; WMEC616 completed
MMA programme in 1990. The B class were Alco
ined from the start. Eight (WMEC620-4/6-7/30) were
nched by American Shipbuilding Company, Lorain,
o between 30 April 1966 and 19 October 1968. Three

were built by the Coast Guard yard, WMEC625 launched
11 November 1967, WMEC628 launched 28 April 1967
and WMEC629 launched 14 December 1967. The MMAs
for the B class were contracted to Colonna's Shipyard at
Norfolk, Va. The first B to undergo MMA was WMEC628
in 1986-7. The programme is due to complete with
WMEC620 at the end of 1990. MMA is designed to
reduce topweight while enlarging the superstructure and
enhancing firefighting capability. The engine uptakes are
being diverted from the stern into a new funnel and the
helicopter deck is being reduced in size. Designed
primarily for search and rescue up to 500 miles off the
coast. They were originally rated Patrol Craft (WPC) but
changed to WMEC in 1966

Photograph: *Diligence* (USNI)
Silhouette: 'Reliance' class pre-MMA

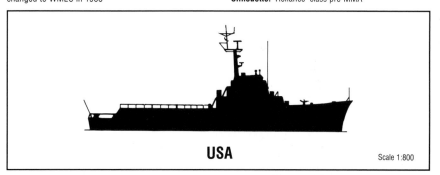

USA

Scale 1:800

Specifications and Technical Data

Displacement, tonnes: 1,947 full load
Dimensions, metres (feet): 70.1 × 13.1 × 4.6 (230 × 43 × 15)
Guns: 1 × 76 mm, 4 × 12.7 mm machine guns
Radar: SPS 64 I band navigation
Machinery: 3 × EMD diesels, 3,000 hp, 1 shaft
Speed, knots: 14
Range, nautical miles: 12,000 at 14 knots, 22,000 at 8 knots
Complement: 106

Originally laid down on 14 July 1941 at the Toledo Shipbuilding Company, Ohio, as the ice patrol tender *Eskimo*, her name was changed while she was still under construction. She was launched on 4 April 1942 and originally carried 2 × 3-inch guns and 4 × 20 mm guns and ASW weapons. She was built for icebreaking and patrol duties in the Greenland area, but in 1949 was transferred to the Pacific for search, rescue and law enforcement duties in Alaskan waters. Given her special utility in these icy waters, she underwent an MMA (Major Maintenance Availablity) refit which was completed in 1986. Her main engines, originally a Fairbanks Morse outfit, were replaced and her living accomodation improved. She was originally rated Icebreaker (WAG/WAGB) but was reclassified Medium Endurance Cutter (WMEC) to reflect her primary law enforcement role. Her main duty is fishery protection. She is expected to remain in service until the mid-1990s, based at Kodiak, Alaska.

Photograph: *Storis* (Chris Stall/USNI)

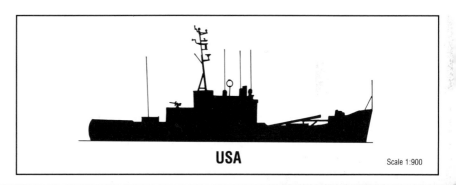

USA

Scale 1:900

Number in class: 5

UTE WMEC76 1942 A
LIPAN WMEC85 1943 A
CHILULA WMEC 153 1945 A
CHEROKEE WMEC165 1940 A
TAMAROA WMEC166 1943 A

Medium Endurance Coast Guard Cutters (WMEC)
Cherokee/Abnaki Class

pecifications
nd Technical Data

placement, tonnes: 1,759 full load
nensions, metres (feet): 62.5 × 11.7 × 5.2
**5 × 38.5 × 17)
ns: 1 × 76 mm, 2 × 40 mm grenade launchers
dar: SPS 64 I band navigation
chinery: 4 × General Motors 12-278 diesels,
**00hp 1 shaft
eed, knots: 16.2
nge, nautical miles: 6,500 at 16 knots,
**000 at 8 knots
mplement: 72

otal of five former large fleet tugs (ATF) were
nsferred to the Coast Guard; three in 1946 on loan and
 more in 1980. The ships on loan were officially
nsferred to the Coast Guard in 1969. WMEC153 and
5 are in reserve after undergoing FRAM (Fleet
nabilitation and Modernisation) refits at the end of the
30s. They were officially rated Medium Endurance
ters on 1 May 1966. WMEC153 was built by the
arleston Shipbuilding and Drydock Company and
nched on 1 Dec 1944. WMEC165 was launched, the
t of her class, by Bethlehem Steel, Statton Island, on
Nov 1939. WMEC166, the last of the class, was
nched by Commercial Iron Works, Portland, Oregon,
 13 July 1943. Her original name was *Zuni*. WMEC76
 85 were both built by United Engineering of
meda, California and launched on 24 June and 17
·t 1942. They were operated by the Military Sealift
nmand until passing to the Coast Guard, and do not
·y 3-inch guns. In addition to these converted tugs,

the Coast Guard also operates the following ships rated as Medium Endurance Cutters — 3 × 1,773 tonne converted salvage ships, *Acushnet* (WMEC167), *Yacona* (WMEC168) and *Escape* (WMEC6), used for tug and oceanographic duties, the first two in the Atlantic and the last in the Pacific; 3 × 1,041 tonne converted seagoing buoy tenders, *Clover* (WMEC292), *Evergreen* (WMEC295) and *Citrus* (WMEC300). WMEC295 is an oceanographic research ship based in the Atlantic, and the other two are stationed in the Pacific for law enforcement duties.

Photograph: *Chilula* (USNI)
Silhouette: *Chilula*

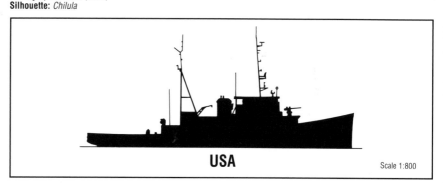

USA

Scale 1:800

Specifications
and Technical Data

Displacement, tonnes: 2,940 submerged
Dimensions, metres (feet): 66.8 × 8.8 × 8.5
(219.1 × 29 × 28)
Torpedo tubes: 6 × 533 mm forward
Sonar: BQR2 passive and BQS active passive search and attack
Radar: BPS 12 I/J band surface search and navigation
Machinery: 3 × Fairbanks Morse 38D8 1/8 diesels, 4,800 hp, 2 × General Electric electric motors, 3,150 hp, 1 × shaft
Speed, knots: 12 surfaced, 21 submerged
Range, nautical miles: about 10,000 miles at 9 knots snorting
Complement: 85

The last conventionally-powered submarine built for the US Navy and the last in sevice. Her two sisters, *Barbel* (SS580) and *Bonefish* (SS582) have been decommissioned for scrap the latter because of bad fire damage in 1988, the former because of serious flooding in heavy weather in the South China Sea in 1989. *Blueback* will decommission in June 1990. These boats had the advanced 'tear-drop' hull form pioneered by the USS *Albacore. Blueback* was laid down by the Ingalls Shipbuilding Corporation on 15 April 1957, launched on 16 May 1959 and was commissioned on 15 October 1959. The bow planes formerly mounted on the hull were later shifted to the sail. These boats pioneered the concept of centralised arrangement of controls in an attack centre. Although not developed further in the United States the design was used as the basis for advanced conventional submarines built in the Netherlands and Japan. USS *Blueback* is armed with the MK 48 heavyweight torpedo. The older conventionally-powered submarine, the USS *Darter*, commissioned in 1956 and based in Japan since 1979 was finally decommissioned at the end of 1989.

Photograph: *Blueback* (USNI)

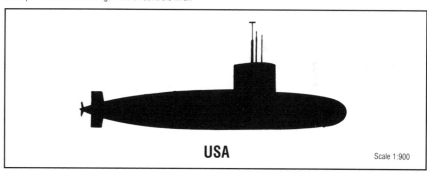

USA

Scale 1:900

ecifications
d Technical Data

placement, tonnes: (LCC19) 18,667,
C20) 18,945 full load
ensions, metres (feet): 194 × 32.9 × 8.8
5.5 × 107.9 × 28.9)
raft: helicopter landing pad aft
siles: 2 × 8 Sea Sparrow amidships
s: 2 × 2 76 mm on each beam forward of bridge,
 20 mm Vulcan Phalanx CIWS fore and aft
tary lift: 700 troops, 3 × LCP, 2 × LCVP
ar: SPS 48C E/F band 3D air search,
 40C E/F band air search, SPS 65 G band surface
 ch, LN 66 I band navigation, Mk 115 I/J band fire
 trol
hinery: 1 × General Electric geared turbine,
 Foster Wheeler boilers, 22,000 hp, 1 × shaft
ed, knots: 23 knots
ge, nautical miles: 13,000 at 16 knots
plement: (LCC19) 799 plus 170 flag staff,
 C20) 777 plus 191 flag staff

e *Ridge* was laid down at the Philadelphia Naval
yard on 27 February 1967 and was launched on
nuary 1969. *Mount Whitney* was laid down
 January 1969 and launched exactly a year later at
Newport News Shipbuilding and Dry Dock Co. Based
he 'Iwo Jima' class LPH hull form with an extra deck
new superstructure, these ships are floating
mand and communication centres reflecting the
plex requirements of controlling of amphibious
rations. They were designed to contain both a Navy
hibious task force command staff and a Marine

assault force command staff. They are fitted with the
Amphibious Command Information System (ACIS) and
the Naval Intelligence Processing System (NIPS) as well
as the Naval Tactical Data System (NTDS). The OE-82
satellite comminications system is mounted on the
prominent 'mack' type structure aft. An important
feature of the design was the provision of deck space for
optimal placing of aerials. Six ships were originally
projected, but instead command capability has been
built into subsequent assault ships and the two LCCs
have changed their role to become the flagships of the
two main operational fleet commanders. *Blue Ridge*
became flagship of the Seventh Fleet in October 1979
and is based at Yokosuka, Japan. *Mount Whitney*

became flagship of the Second Fleet at Norfolk, Virginia,
in January 1981. She regularly deploys as flagship of the
NATO Striking Fleet Atlantic. These fleet command ships
are to be modernised with a new Tactical Flag Command
Center and to be protected with Kevlar armour

Photograph: *Mount Whitney* 1980 (Bob Simms/USNI)

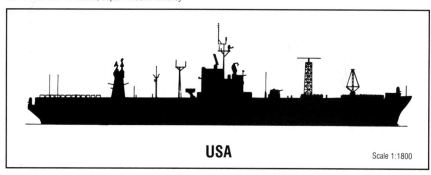

USA

Scale 1:1800

Number in class: 5

WASP LHD1 1989 A
ESSEX LHD2 1992
KEARSAGE LHD3 1993
BOXER LHD4 1994
LHD5

Amphibious Assault Ships (LHD)
Wasp Class

pecifications
nd Technical Data

placement, tonnes: 41,183 full load
nensions, metres (feet): 257.3 × 42.7 × 8.1
4 × 140.1 × 26.6)
craft: up to 32 CH-46 helicopters and 6 AV-8B
riers or 20 AV-8B Harriers and up to 6 SH-60B ASW
copters
ssiles: 2 × 8 Sea Sparrow on forward superstructure
at stern
ns: 3 × 20 mm Vulcan Phalanx CIWS, one on forward
erstructure, two on stern
itary lift: 1,873 troops, 3 × LCAC air cushion
icles or 12 × LCM 6
dar: (LHD1) SPS 52C, (remainder) SPS48 E E/F band
search, SPS 49(V)5 C/D band air search, SPS 67 G
d surface search, SPS I/band navigation, SPN 45 and
I band carrier approach aid, Mk 23 D band Target
quisition System
ion Information Organisation: SYS 2(V) 3
chinery: 2 × Westinghouse geared turbines,
Combustion Engineering boilers, 70,000 hp,
shafts
eed, knots: 23
nge, nautical miles: 9,500 at 18 knots
mplement: 1,080

ge and impressive carrier-type vessels that combine
stantial aviation facilities with a well deck and the
acity to land heavy equipment either by conventional
ding craft or air-cushion vehicle. There are nine
copter landing spots on the flight deck, which has
been given a ski jump in order to optimise helicopter

operations. The ships are based on the previous LHAs
but with a revised docking well to accommodate LCACs,
a revised elevator layout and increased support capacity
for AV-8B STOV/L aircraft. The stern gate is a normal
LSD/LPD type rather than the rising sectional gate of the
LHAs. Cargo capacity is 2,860 cubic metres
(101,000 cubic feet) and 623 square metres
(22,000 square feet) of vehicle storage space. The ships
are being constructed by the Ingalls Shipbuilding
Division of Litton Industries of Pascagoula, Mississippi.
Wasp was begun on 30 May 1985 and launched on 4
August 1987. She was commissioned in May 1989.
LHD2 and LHD3 were both begun in 1989 and LHD4 was
ordered in October 1988. LHD5 is being requested in the

Fiscal 1991 programme. The ships can support a large
number of different types of aircraft including the AH-1W
Super Cobra, the AH-1T Sea Cobra, the CH-53E Super
Stallion, the CH-53D Sea Stallion and the UH-1 Huey.
They have an important secondary role as ASW/STOV/L
carriers in the sea control role and are highly flexible
units. The ships cost in the region of $750 to $800
million.

Photograph: *Wasp* 1989 (Ingalls Shipbuilding/USNI)

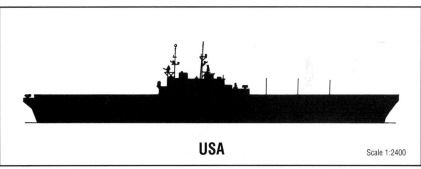

USA

Scale 1:2400

Number in class: 5

TARAWA LHA1 1976 P
SAIPAN LHA2 1977 A
BELLEAU WOOD LHA3 1978 P
NASSAU LHA4 1979 A
PELELIU LHA5 1980 P

Amphibious Assault Ships (LHA)
Tarawa Class

pecifications
nd Technical Data

placement, tonnes: 39,931 full load
nensions, metres (feet): 254.2 × 40.2 × 7.9
4 × 131.9 × 25.9)
craft: 16 × CH-46, 6 × CH-53, 4 × UH-1,
V-8B Harriers
ssiles: 2 × 8 Sea Sparrow on forward superstructure
d at stern (being removed)
ns: 2 × 127 mm at bow, 6 × 20 mm, 2 × 20 mm
can Phalanx CIWS replacing Sea Sparrow
litary lift: about 1,900 troops, 4 × LCU 1610,
to 6 smaller landing craft
dar: SPS 52C E/F band 3D air search, SPS 40B E/F
nd air search, SPS 10F G band surface search, LN 66 I
nd navigation, SPN 35 I band carrier approach aid,
G 60 and SPQ 9A I/J band fire control
ion Information Organisation: ITAWDS
chinery: 2 × Westinghouse geared turbines,
× Combustion Engineering boilers, 70,000 hp,
× shafts,
) hp bow thruster
eed, knots: 24
nge, nautical miles: 10,000 at 20 knots
nplement: 940

ovel combination of LPD, LPH and LKA , these ships
e built using equally innovative modular shipbuilding
nniques by the Ingalls Shipbuilding Division of Litton
ustries of Pascagoula, Mississippi. Construction of
h ship began on 15 November 1971, 21 July 1972,
larch 1973, 13 August 1973, 12 November 1976.
y were launched on 1 December 1973, 18 July 1974,

11 April 1977, 12 January 1978 and 25 November 1978.
The mix of aircraft can be altered according to mission.
There is 3,310 cubic metres (116,900 cubic feet) of
stores space and 956 square metres (33,730 square
feet) of vehicle storage space. Effectively, each ship
can carry and land a reinforced Marine battalion as well
as give them air support with up to twenty Harriers.
The dock is 82 metres (268 feet) long and 24 metres
(78 feet) wide, can take four LCUs, but only one LCAC.
Alternative combinations of landing craft can be
accommodated in the dock, e.g. 2 LCUs and 3 LCM-8s,
17 LCM 6s or 45 LVTP-7 amphibious tractors, 34 of the
latter can also be accommodated internally. A large fully
equipped hospital is also carried. The 5-inch guns are

intended primarily to give fire support for the troops.
The ships are also intended to carry and operate
reconnaissance drones. They carry a full EW fit with four
SRBOC flare and chaff launchers and the SLQ 32(V)3
combined ESM/ECM. LHA5 was originally to be named
Darnang.

Photograph: *Nassau* (Litton Shipbuilding/USNI)

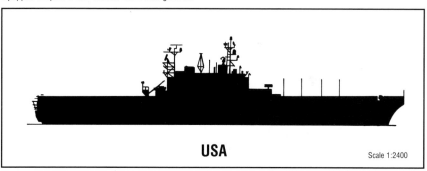

USA

Scale 1:2400

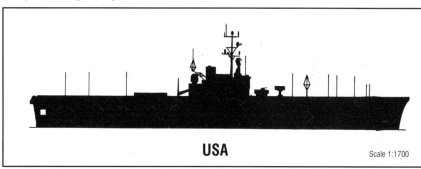

Number in class: 7

IWO JIMA LPH2 1961 A
OKINAWA LPH3 1962 P
GUADALCANAL LPH7 1963 A
GUAM LPH9 1965 A
TRIPOLI LPH10 1966 P
NEW ORLEANS LPH11 1968 P
INCHON LPH12 1970 A

ɔecifications
d Technical Data

placement, tonnes: 18,594 full load
ɹensions, metres (feet): 183.7 × 31.7 × 7.9
2. × 104 × 26)
:raft: 20 × CH-46 helicopters, 4 × AV-8B Harriers
siles: (except LPH3) 2 × 8 Sea Sparrow forward of
ɘerstructure and on port quarter
ɪs: 2 × 2 76 mm forward of bridge and on starboard
rter, 2 × 20 mm Vulcan Phalanx CIWS on each beam
ɪtary lift: 2,000 troops, (LPH12) 2 × LCVP
ɑr: SPS 58 D band 3D air search, SPS 40 E/F band
search, SPS 10 G band surface search, SPN 35 and
ᴎ band carrier approach aid, LN 66 I band navigation,
115 I/J band fire control
ɔhinery: 1 × De Laval or General Electric or
stinghouse geared turbine, 2 × Babcock and Wilcox
Combustion Engineering boilers, 22,000 hp.
: shaft
ɘed, knots: 23
ɪge, nautical miles: 10,000 at 20 knots
nplement: 685

 LPH concept was developed for 'vertical
ɘelopment', ie helicopter assault. The first LPH was a
ɪverted escort carrier, but it was decided in 1957 to
 d ships specially for the role as well as convert old
t carriers. Later 'Iwo Jimas' replaced the converted
iers. The LPHs can also be used for other duties.
ᴎ9 operated as a Sea Control Ship (SCS) from
2-74 flying a mix of Harrier fighters and Sea King
ᴎ helicopters and ships of this class have also been
d to carry and operate RH-53 minesweeping

helicopters. Up to eleven large CH-53 helicopters can be
carried instead of the CH-46 aircraft. They are effectively
small multi-purpose aircraft carriers. LPH2 was built at
the Puget Sound Naval Shipyard, being laid down on
2 April 1959 and launched on 17 September 1960.
LPH3, LPH7, LPH9 and LPH11 were all built in the
Philadelphia Naval Shipyard, being laid down on 1 April
1960, 1 September 1961, 15 November 1962 and
1 March 1966. They were launched on 14 August 1961,
16 March 1963, 22 August 1964 and 3 February 1968.
LPH10 and LPH12 were built by Ingalls Shipbuilding at
Pascagoula, being laid down on 15 June 1964 and
8 April 1968. They were launched on 31 July 1965 and
24 May 1969. Stowage capacity is 1,059 cubic metres

(37,400 cubic feet) of stores and 122 square metres
(4,300 square feet) for vehicles. The ships are intended
to be able to land a battalion landing team by helicopter.
There are full medical facilities on board. The ships carry
the normal EW fit of four SRBOC flare and chaff
launchers and the SLQ 33(V)3 combined ESM/ECM.

Photograph: *Guadalcanal* 1987 (USNI)

USA

Scale 1:1700

AUSTIN LPD4 1965 A
OGDEN LPD5 1965 P
DULUTH LPD6 1965 P
CLEVELAND LPD7 1967 P
DUBUQUE LPD8 1967 P
DENVER LPD9 1968 P
JUNEAU LPD10 1969 P

CORONADO AGF11 1970 P
SHREVEPORT LPD12 1970 A
NASHVILLE LPD13 1970 A
TRENTON LPD14 1971 A
PONCE LPD15 1971 A

Amphibious Transport Docks and Miscellaneous Command Ships (LPD/AGF)
Austin Class

Specifications and Technical Data

Displacement, tonnes: 17,171 full load
Dimensions, metres (feet): 173.8 × 30.5 × 7
(570 c 100 × 23)
Aircraft: up to 6 SH-46D/E Sea Knight helicopters
Guns: 1-2 × 2 76 mm, 2 × 20 mm Vulcan Phalanx
CWS
Military lift: 840-930 troops, 9 × LCM 6 or 4 × LCM 8
Radar: SPS 40B/C E/F band air search, SPS 10F
or SPS 67 G band surface search, LN 66 navigation
Machinery: 2 × De Laval steam turbines, 2 × Foster
Wheeler or Babcock and Wilcox boilers, 24,000 hp,
2 × shafts
Speed, knots: 21
Range, nautical miles: 7,700 at 20 knots
Complement: 420, (AGF11) 516, (LPD7-13),
(AGF11) 90 flag staff

The LPD combines the roles of assault transport and
dock landing ship. Compared to equivalent LSDs they
have a smaller docking well and additional space for
troops and vehicles. LPD7-13 were fitted out as
flagships and, in 1980, *Coronado* was re-rated
Miscellaneous Command Ship (AGF) in order to take up
temporary duty as flagship of the Commander Middle
East Force. She later served as flagship in the
Mediterranean and in 1986 took up her current duty a
flagship of the Third Fleet based at Pearl Harbour. She
retains her amphibious capability if required. The dock
area can accommodate two LCAC air-cushion vehicles.
The ships carry a telescopic hangar for a small utility

helicopter (a Sea King in *Coronado*) but can operate six
transport helicopters as a deck park for short periods.
LPD4-6 were built by New York Naval Shipyard, the first
two were both laid down and launched on the same
days, 4 February 1963 and 27 June 1964. LPD6 was laid
down on 18 December 1963 and launched on 14 August
1965, LPD7-8 were both built by the Ingalls Shipbuilding
Corporation, being laid down on 30 November 1964 and
25 January 1965 and launched on 23 January 1965 and
12 February 1966. The final six ships were all built by the
Lockheed Shipbuilding and Construction Company of
Seattle, being laid down on 7 February 1964,
23 January 1965, 3 May 1965, 27 December 1965,
14 March 1966, 8 August 1966 and 31 October 1966.

These ships were launched on 23 January 1965,
12 February 1966, 30 July 1966, 25 October 1966,
7 October 1967, 3 August 1968 and 30 May 1970.

Photograph: *Cleveland* 1981 (USNI)

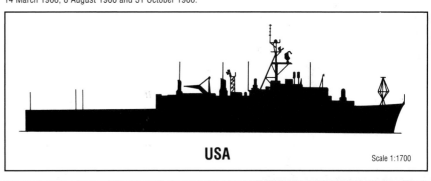

USA

Scale 1:1700

RALEIGH LPD1 1962 A
VANCOUVER LPD2 1963 P
LA SALLE AGF3 1964 A

pecifications
nd Technical Data

splacement, tonnes: (LPD1) 13,818, (LPD2) 14,900,
GF3) 14,885 full load
mensions, metres (feet): 159.1 × 30.5 × 6.7
21.8 × 100 × 22)
rcraft: up to 6 × CH-46 Sea Knight helicopters
ns: 2-3 × 2 76 mm, 2 × 20 mm Vulcan Phalanx
WS
litary lift: 930 troops, 1 × LCU, 3 × LCM 6
dar: SPS 40 E/F band air search, SPS 10 G band
rface search, LN 66 I band navigation
achinery: 2 × De Laval geared turbines, 2 × Babcock
d Wilcox boilers, 24,000 hp, 2 × shafts
eed, knots: 21
nge, nautical miles: 9,600 at 16 knots
mplement: 430

The prototype LPD class, built at New York Naval
Shipyard, being laid down on 23 June 1960,
19 November 1960 and 2 April 1962. They were
launched on 17 March 1962, 15 September 1962 and
24 February 1964. They were intended to replace both
the amphibious transport (LPA) and the dock landing
ship (LSD). They were designed with greater cargo
carrying capacity than previous LSDs and the docking
well is only 51.2 metres (168 feet) long and 15.2 metres
(50 feet) wide. The design was lengthened slightly in the
suceeding 'Austin' class which have a dock 120 metres
(394 feet) long. The 'Raleighs' are being modified to
carry an LCAC. In 1972 *La Salle* was re-rated
Miscellaneous Command Ship (AGF) for duty in the

Persian Gulf. With a short break for overhaul in 1980-82
she has been flagship for the Command US Middle East
Force. She has a hangar for a Sea King helicopter and a
shelter covering part of the flight deck. Additional
air-conditioning is fitted and she is painted white. The
pair of 'Raleigh' class LPDs will serve until the late
1990s when they will be replaced by the cargo variant of
the 'Whidbey Island' class.

Photograph: *Vancouver* (USNI)
Silhouette: *La Salle*

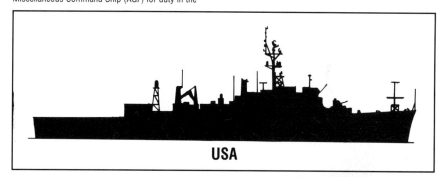

USA

Number in class: 13

WHIDBEY ISLAND LSD41 1985 A
GERMANTOWN LSD42 1986 P
FORT McHENRY LSD43 1987 P
GUNSTON HALL LSD44 1989 A
COMSTOCK LSD45 1989
TORTUGA LSD46 1989
RUSHMORE LSD47 1990

ASHLAND LSD48 1990
HARPERS FERRY LSD49 1993
LSD50
LSD51
LSD52
LSD53

pecifications
d Technical Data

placement, tonnes: 15,978 full load
tensions, metres (feet): 185.6 × 25.6 × 6.3
9 × 84 × 20.5)
raft: 2 landing spots for medium to large helicopters
is: 2 × 20 mm Vulcan Phalanx CIWS, 2 × 25
'0 mm, 8 × 12.7 mm machine guns
itary lift: 450 troops, 4 × LCAC or 21 × LCM 6
× LCU
lar: SPS 49(V) C/D band air search, SPS 67(V) G
d surface search, SPS 64 I/J band navigation
chinery: 4 × Colt-Pielstick 16 PC25-V400 diesels,
i00 hp, 2 × shafts
ed, knots: 22
ge, nautical miles: 8,000 at 18 knots
nplement: 340

ed on the previous 'Anchorage' class of LSDs these
s emphasise dock capacity. The well deck is 134.1
res (440 feet) by 15.2 metres (50 feet) and is
nded primarily for the operation of LCAC air-cushion
ing craft. The helicopter platform is raised in order
rovide ventilation for their gas turbine engines. The
s have a cargo capacity of 141.6 cubic metres
00 cubic feet) for marine cargo and 1,214 square
res (13,068 square feet) of vehicle parking space.
pers Ferry (LSD49) onwards will be built to a special
go variant' design with 1,133 cubic metres (40,000
c feet) of space for marine cargo. Full load
placement will be marginally increased to 16,963

tonnes. The first three ships were built by Lockheed
Shipbuilding of Seattle, being laid down on
4 August 1981, 5 August 1982 and 19 June 1983. They
were launched 10 June 1983, 29 June 1984 and
1 February 1986. The rest of the class have so far been
laid down at Avondale Shipyards, New Orleans. Laying
down dates were 29 May 1986, 27 October 1986,
23 March 1987, 9 November 1987 and 4 April 1988.
LSD 44-8 were launched in June 1987, January 1988,
June 1988, September 1988, February 1989 and July
1989. LSD49 first of the modified ships, is due to be laid
down in April 1991. It is hoped to have all the modified
ships funded by Fiscal 1992. LSD44 onwards have NBC
(Nuclear Biological Chemical) protection systems.

Photograph: *Fort McHenry* 1987 (Lockheed
Shipbuilding/USNI)

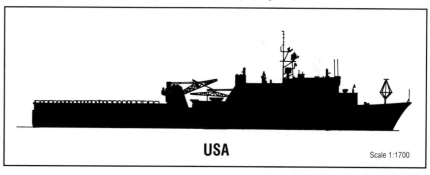

USA

Scale 1:1700

ANCHORAGE LSD36 1969 P
PORTLAND LSD37 1970 A
PENSACOLA LSD38 1971 A
MOUNT VERNON LSD 39 1972 P
FORT FISHER LSD40 1972 P

Specifications
and Technical Data

Displacement, tonnes: 13,920 full load
Dimensions, metres (feet): 168.6 × 25.6 × 6
(53.3 × 84 × 20)
Aircraft: removeable helicopter platform aft
Guns: 2 × 2 76 mm, 2 × 20 mm Vulcan Phalanx CIWS
Military lift: 366 troops, 3 × LCU, 2 × LCM 6
Radar: SPS 40 E/F band air search, SPS 10 G band
surface search. LN 66 I band navigation
Machinery: 2 × De Laval geared turbines,
2 × Combustion Engineering or Foster Wheeler boilers,
24,000 hp, 2 × shafts
Speed, knots: 22 knots
Complement: 358

Built to complement the previous LPDs in order to increase the number of landing craft available for an amphibious assault. The docking well is 131.1 metres (430 feet) long and 15.2 metres (50 feet) wide. The ships have 1,115 square metres (12,000 square feet) of vehicle parking space forward of the well deck. Instead of the LCUs the well can contain fifty LCM 6s, eight LCM 8s or fifty LVTs. The two additional LCM 6s are stowed on deck and lifted by 50 foot cranes. LSD36 was built by the Ingalls Shipbuilding Corporation, being laid down on 13 March 1967 and launched on 5 May 1968. LSD37-40 were all built by General Dynamics of Quincy, Mass. and were laid down on 21 September 1967,

12 March 1969, 29 January 1970 and 15 July 1970. They were launched on 20 December 1969, 11 July 1970, 17 April 1971 and 22 April 1972. The ships were originally armed with four twin 76 mm mountings but these have been progressively removed. The ships have been fitted with a modern EW fit, four SRBOC six-barrelled flare and chaff rocket launchers and the SLQ 32(V)1 ESM.

Photograph: *Portland* 1986 (van Ginderern/USNI)

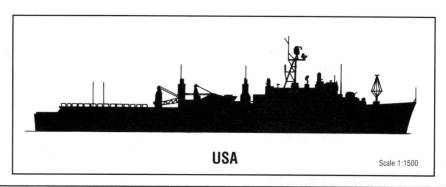

USA

Scale 1:1500

THOMASTON LSD28 1954 P
PLYMOUTH ROCK LSD29 1954 A
FORT SNELLING LSD30 1955 A
POINT DEFIANCE LSD31 1955 P

SPIEGEL GROVE LSD32 1956 A
ALAMO LSD33 1956 P
HERMITAGE LSD34 1956 A
MONTICELLO LSD35 1957 P

ecifications
d Technical Data

lacement, tonnes: 12,345 full load
ensions, metres (feet): 155.5 × 25.6 × 5.8
⬤ × 84 × 19)
raft: removeable helicopter platform aft
s: 2 × 3 76 mm, 2 × 20 mm Vulcan Phalanx CIWS
ary lift: 340 troops, 3 × LCU or 9 × LCM8
⬤ LCM 6
ar: SPS 6 L band air search, SPS 10 G band surface
ch, LN 66 I/J band navigation
hinery: 2 × General Electric geared turbines,
Babcock and Wilcox boilers, 24,000 hp, 2 × shafts
ed, knots: 22.5
ge, nautical miles: 10,000 at 20 knots
plement: 348

Built in the 1950s as a result of the vindication of
amphibious operations in the Korean War these ships
were logical development of the British-inspired wartime
LSD concept. Only LSD32-34 remain in service, the rest
are in reserve; Pacific ships at Bremerton, Washington,
and Atlantic ships at Portsmouth, Virginia. They are
being replaced by the 'Whidbey Island' class and USS
Alamo is being transferred to Brazil. They were originally
armed with eight twin 76 mm mountings and twelve 20
mm guns but this was progressively reduced from the
1960s onwards. CIWS was added to active ships in the
1980s. The well deck is 119.2 metres (391 feet) long
and 14.6 metres (48 feet) wide. The ships have
975 square metres (10,495 square feet) of vehicle

parking space. They were all built by Ingalls Shipbuilding
of Pascagoula and were laid down on 3 March 1953,
5 May 1953, 17 August 1953, 23 November 1953,
7 September 1954, 11 October 1954, 11 April 1955 and
6 June 1955. They were launched on 9 February, 1954,
7 May 1954, 16 July 1954, 28 September 1954,
10 November 1955, 20 January 1956, 12 June 1956 and
10 August 1956.

Photograph: *Thomaston* (USNI)

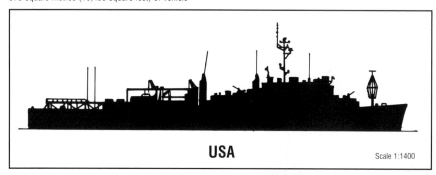

USA

Scale 1:1400

NEWPORT LST1179 1969 A
MANITOWOC LST1180 1970 A
SUMTER LST1181 1970 A
FRESNO LST1182 1969 P
PEORIA LST1183 1970 P
FREDERICK LST1184 1970 P
SCHENECTADY LST1185 1970 P

CAYUGA LST1186 1970 P
TUSCALOOSA LST1187 1970 P
SAGINAW LST1188 1971 A
SAN BERNARDINO LST1189 1971 P
BOULDER LST1190 1971 A
RACINE LST1191 1971 P

SPARTANBURG COUNTY LST1192 1971 A
FAIRFAX COUNTY LST1193 1971 A
LA MOURE COUNTY LST1194 1971 A
BARBOUR COUNTY LST1195 1972 P

HARLAN COUNTY LST1196 1972 A
BARNSTABLE COUNTY LST1197 1972 A
BRISTOL COUNTY LST1198 1972 P

Displacement, tonnes: 8,586 full load
Dimensions, metres (feet): 159.2 × 21.2 × 5.3 (522.3 × 69.5 × 17.5)
Aircraft: helicopter platform
Guns: 2 × 276 mm on each side of bridge, 1 × 20 mm Vulcan Phalanx CIWS above bridge
Military lift: 400 troops, 508 tonnes of vehicles, 1 LCVP
Radar: SPS 10F G band surface search being replaced by SPS 67, LN 66 I band or (LST1188/1192-4) Pathfinder I/J band navigation
Machinery: 6 × General Motors or Alco diesels, 16,000 hp, 2 × shafts, bow thruster
Speed, knots: 20
Range, nautical miles: 2,500 at 14 knots
Complement: 253

A revolutionary class of fast oceangoing tank landing ships, these were built to combine a beaching capability for the landing of heavy vehicles with an ability to operate with 20 knot amphibious task forces. Unlike other landing ships they did not have opening bows, but instead have a 34 metre (112 feet) bow ramp operated by a prominent derrick which allows vehicles to be landed over their bow. There is also a stern ramp that allows amphibious vehicles to be offloaded directly into the water or other vehicles to be transferred into smaller landing craft. The ships can also carry up to four pontoon sections for unloading without beaching. The LCVPs are on davits amidships. The ships have 1,765

square metres (17,300 square feet) of vehicle parking area. The first three were built by the Philadelphia Naval Shipyard being laid down between November 1966 and November 1967. They were launched on 3 February 1968, 4 June 1969 and 13 June 1969. The rest were all built by the National Steel and Shipbuilding Company of San Diego, California being laid down between December 1967 and February 1971. They were launched between 28 September 1968 and 4 December 1971. Two of the class, LST1190 and LST1191, were transferred to the Naval Reserve Force in 1980-81. These ships form vital components of amphibious task forces which otherwise would only be able to land the heaviest combat and engineering equipment with great difficulty.

A number of older tank landing ships remain in the mercantile National Defense Reserve Fleet but their mobilisation is unlikely.

Photograph: *Peoria* 1989 (USNI)

USA

Scale 1:1500

CHARLESTON LKA113 1968 A
DURHAM LKA114 1969 A
MOBILE LKA115 1969 P
ST. LOUIS LKA116 1969 P
EL PASO LKA117 1970 A

pecifications
nd Technical Data

splacement, tonnes: 21,032
nensions, metres (feet): 175.4 × 18.9 × 7.7
*5.5 × 62 × 25.6)
craft: helicopter landing pad aft
ns: (LKA113/117) 2, (remainder) 3 × 2.76 mm in
w and beside bridge; (LKA113/117) portside only,
KA113/117 only) 2 × 20 mm Vulcan Phalanx CIWS
ward and on starboard side of bridge
itary lift: 362 troops, 4 × LCM 8, 5 × LCM 6,
× LCVPs, 2 × LCP
dar: SPS 10 F G band surface search being replaced
SPS 67, LN 66 (LKA113 only) Pathfinder I band
igation
chinery: 1 × Westinghouse steam turbine,
 Combustion Engineering boilers, 19,250 hp,
 shaft
eed, knots: 20
mplement: 360

 down at the Newport News Shipbuilding Company
ween 5 December 1966 and 22 October 1969 to
vide 20 knot amphibious groups with munitions and
visions. These can be landed either by helicopter
ng the pad aft or by landing craft, up to nine of which
carried fore and aft of the superstructure. The ships
e launched on 2 December 1967, 29 March 1968,
October 1968, 4 January 1969 and 17 May 1969.
Louis is forward based at Sasebo, Japan. The other
 were transferred to the Naval Reserve Force

between 1979 and 1981 but they were returned to the
active fleet in 1982-83 in order to improve amphibious
readiness. The ships have 1,982 cubic metres
(70,000 cubic feet) of cargo space and 3,066 square
metres (33,000 square feet) of vehicle storage space.
They have two 79 tonne capacity cranes, two 40 tonne
capacity booms and eight 15 tonne capacity booms for
unloading into landing craft alongside. These ships were
originally ordered as Attack Cargo Ships (AKA) but the
designation was changed to the current on 14 December
1968 when *Charleston* was commissioned. Despite their
mercantile appearance these are as much major
warships as any of the other members of the powerful
American amphibious fleet.

Photograph: *Durham* 1989 (Paul Self/USNI)

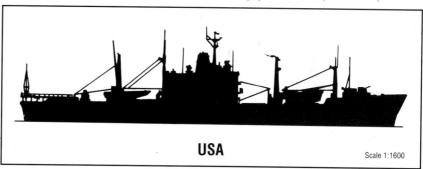

USA

Scale 1:1600

ndex of
ennant Numbers

SSN699, 21
SSN700, 21
SSN701, 21
SSN702, 21
SSN703, 21
SSN704, 21
SSN705, 21
SSN706, 21
SSN707, 21
SSN708, 21
SSN709, 21
SSN710, 21
SSN711, 21
SSN712, 21
SSN713, 21
SSN714, 21
SSN715, 21
SSN716, 21
SSN717, 21
SSN718, 21
SSN719, 21
SSN720, 21
SSN721, 21
SSN722, 21
SSN723, 21
SSN724, 21
SSN725, 21
SSN750, 21
SSN751, 21
SSN752, 21
SSN753, 21
SSN754, 21
SSN755, 21

SSN756, 21
SSN757, 21
SSN758, 21
SSN759, 21
SSN760, 21
SSN761, 21
SSN762, 21
SSN763, 21
SSN764, 21
SSN765, 21
SSN766, 21
SSN767, 21
SSN768, 21
SSN769, 21
SSN770, 21
SSN771, 21
SSN772, 21
SSN773, 21
WHEC715, 91
WHEC716, 91
WHEC717, 91
WHEC718, 91
WHEC719, 91
WHEC720, 91
WHEC721, 91
WHEC722, 91
WHEC723, 91
WHEC724, 91
WHEC725, 91
WHEC726, 91
WMEC38, 97
WMEC76, 99
WMEC85, 99

WMEC153, 99
WMEC165, 99
WMEC166, 99
WMEC615, 95
WMEC616, 95
WMEC617, 95
WMEC618, 95
WMEC619, 95
WMEC620, 95
WMEC621, 95
WMEC622, 95
WMEC623, 95
WMEC624, 95
WMEC625, 95
WMEC626, 95
WMEC627, 95
WMEC628, 95
WMEC629, 95
WMEC630, 95
WMEC901, 93
WMEC902, 93
WMEC903, 93
WMEC904, 93
WMEC905, 93
WMEC906, 93
WMEC907, 93
WMEC908, 93
WMEC909, 93
WMEC910, 93
WMEC911, 93
WMEC912, 93
WMEC913, 93